KV-190-449

Perfect parties

GW 3137924 9

one good idea can change your life...

Perfect parties

High-performance entertaining to enchant your guests

Lizzie O'Prey

CAREFUL NOW

It's your party and you can cry if you want to.

The party animals at Infinite Ideas have done everything they can to make your party a success, and we genuinely hope you have a ball. You can't always make whoopee without breaking a few eggs, however, and so we have to remind you that hangovers, drunken rows, red-wine stains, cigarette burns and regrettable sexual encounters are just some of the risks of partying (and that's on a good night). Sorry as we are for any damage done we have to remind you that you're a grown-up now, and while this book is full of ideas for you, the responsibility for putting them into practice is entirely your own. We love you, but we're not coming round to clear up in the morning. Besides, we don't recall being invited.

Party on.

Copyright © The Infinite Ideas Company Limited, 2005

The right of Lizzie O'Prey to be identified as the author of this book has been asserted in accordance with the Copyright, Designs and Patents Act 1988.

First published in 2005 by
The Infinite Ideas Company Limited
36 St Giles
Oxford
OX1 3LD
United Kingdom
www.infideas.com

All rights reserved. Except for the quotation of small passages for the purposes of criticism and review, no part of this publication may be reproduced, stored in a retrieval system or transmitted in any form or by any means, electronic, mechanical, photocopying, recording, scanning or otherwise, except under the terms of the Copyright, Designs and Patents Act 1988 or under the terms of a licence issued by the Copyright Licensing Agency Ltd, 90 Tottenham Court Road, London W1T 4LP, UK, without the permission in writing of the publisher. Requests to the publisher should be addressed to the Permissions Department, Infinite Ideas Limited, 36 St Giles, Oxford OX1 3LD, UK or faxed to +44 (0)1865 514777.

A CIP catalogue record for this book is available from the British Library.

ISBN 1-904902-28-6

Brand and product names are trademarks or registered trademarks of their respective owners.

Designed and typeset by Baseline Arts Ltd, Oxford
Printed and bound by TJ International, Cornwall

Brilliant ideas

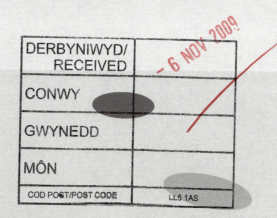

DERBYNIWYD/ RECEIVED	~ 6 NOV 2009
CONWY	
GWYNEDD	
MÔN	
COD POST/POST CODE	LL5 1AS

Brilliant features

Each chapter of this book is designed to provide you with an inspirational idea that you can read quickly and put into practice straight away.

Throughout you'll find four features that will help you get right to the heart of the idea:

■ *Here's an idea for you* Take it on board and give it a go – right here, right now. Get an idea of how well you're doing so far.

■ *Try another idea* If this idea looks like a life-changer then there's no time to lose. *Try another idea* will point you straight to a related tip to enhance and expand on the first.

■ *Defining idea* Words of wisdom from masters and mistresses of the art, plus some interesting hangers-on.

■ *How did it go?* If at first you do succeed, try to hide your amazement. If, on the other hand, you don't, then this is where you'll find a Q and A that highlights common problems and how to get over them.

Introduction

In the immortal words of Madonna: 'Where's the party, I want to free my soul, Where's the party, I want to lose control...'

Now, in certain situations it's all very well to cut loose, but if truth be told you will only feel relaxed enough to do that when you are happy with your preparations for an event. The keyword for successful entertaining is this: plan. It might involve drawing up a guest list or booking a venue. It could incorporate ordering food, finding a band or a DJ, or decorating the place you are holding your party. When you start to think about organising entertainment or hosting an event of any kind, there is inevitably a long list of details to consider.

Organisation ... that doesn't sound like a whole lot of fun. Well, I can't guarantee that everything to do with entertaining is a barrel of laughs, but most of it can be enjoyable when you approach it with a positive attitude. Don't allow yourself to view planning a party or setting up a social situation as a chore. Instead, why not relish the opportunity to be responsible for a whole lot of people having a great deal of fun? (That should include you, by the way.) Make it your mission to address the planning at the earliest possible opportunity so that everything is arranged well in advance. Then you can relax and party without any anxieties.

Can I offer a little inspiration to help you with your endeavours?

Imagine your delight, at the end of the night, when people say thank you for an unforgettable evening (coordinated by you know who!). Think how amazing it will be when they're still talking about 'that fantastic party' weeks afterwards. Consider the fun you'll have when everyone at the party can't resist the chance to get up and dance (when it was you who specifically asked the DJ to include that particular track in his playlist). Just think how much satisfaction you will get from watching your guests gaze in amazement at a stunning ice sculpture – the centrepiece for the buffet (and all your idea).

You may think that some of these ideas are unachievable. You are wrong. They are all well within your capabilities. If I can do it, then anybody can. But these things don't happen by chance. So please use this book as a source of hints, tips and advice to help make entertaining, in all its many forms, that much easier. Incidentally, it will also help you become the ideal guest, the person everyone wants to invite.

Read on and let these ideas inspire you. They could give you the confidence to stock your bar with a great mix of drinks, put together an outfit that will knock someone's socks off (metaphorically speaking, unless you get lucky, of course), request all the right tunes for the disco or even have your speech well prepared and thoroughly rehearsed before you take centre stage.

I want you to have fun at both casual and formal events. So there are guidelines for planning and attending both types of parties. I want you to be able to enjoy an affair that involves every generation of your family from the oldest grandparent, or even great-grandparent, down to the youngest tiny baby or toddler. I hope I've given you enough information to help you handle people of every age.

Are you worried that you'll say or do the wrong thing when meeting people for the first time? Then taking a little advice on the etiquette of certain situations may settle your nerves and ensure that you are the life and soul of the party. Have you always wanted to be a cocktail queen, but never got around to mixing anything more than a whisky and water? Then there is some useful information here that will point you in the right direction. If you find yourself thinking that you would like to spend more time entertaining at home, then read on. If you're single and you'd like to be more comfortable walking into a party full of couples, or just people who already know each other, then put into practice some of the advice that follows.

This book is designed to bring you the best of party planning, be it for colleagues, friends or family, and it includes useful guidance on how much and what kind of food and drink you might consider serving when you are entertaining. Bear in mind that if you consult an expert party planner they might see things differently; should you talk to a proficient chef or a professional barperson you will have the chance to consider advice from a different point of view. When you start to enjoy certain aspects of entertaining, you will certainly want to acquire as much specialist knowledge as you can.

Finally, and most of all, drink within your limits, act your age (for the most part) and get set to enjoy the party!

All fired up

There's the promise of a sun-filled day and you get the feeling that you want to entertain – summer's here and it's the season to barbecue.

When the weather is bright and you are in the mood to socialise, then the time is right to eat alfresco. But let's be realistic about cooking outside.

Very few people take the time to learn the most basic skills. However, they're so simple that it seems ridiculous to suffer burnt sausages or undercooked chicken, blackened fish and shrivelled burgers.

Timing is everything. So, while you don't need to approach it like a military operation, it is an idea to have a plan for the hour or two that precedes the arrival of your guests. Have meat already marinating, have lights set up ready for when the sun goes down, have seats in sociable groups around the patio and have salads prepared. Let's consider the elements that make up the perfect barbecue.

Here's an idea for you…

Cleaning a barbecue ranks alongside going to the recycling bank as one of those chores you put off for days but know you've got to face one day. Make sure that leftover charcoal is removed on a regular basis and cut down on the worst of the cooking detritus by lining grates with foil. Remember to soak them in soapy water after the unit has cooled.

TYPE OF BARBECUE

Do you want to cook by gas or charcoal? It's probably just me, but cooking by gas always seems to be the cheat's way out. If you look at it in terms of restaurants, then a gas barbecue is a perfectly respectable but uninspiring bistro while a charcoal grill is more of a quality, five-star affair. I know people who are perfectly happy with gas and say how easy it is to get the grill going and cook food without burning it – but don't wimp out. Some things in life present a challenge and perfecting the art of cooking with a charcoal grill is one of them. The object of the exercise is to enjoy the food, after all, and the smoked-in taste of 'genuine' barbecue food only comes with a real fire. The Rolls Royce of the barbecue world is a Charcoal Weber and it's worth every penny (even if it does spend several months of the year parked in the garage).

GUESTS

You need to have a rough idea of numbers in order to buy the right amount of food. Two to three portions of meat per person, or two of meat and one of fish, is a good guide.

FOOD

Are you having standard barbecue fare or are you going to put together something more interesting? Think marinated fish kebabs, garlic prawns and stuffed tomatoes. If you buy a decent barbecue you'll get some recipes in the manual but do take the time to search around for more unusual ones. Once you have become governor of your grill you can cook sweet and savoury, small portions and whole joints – so don't just stick to sausages and burgers and hot dogs every time you fire up.

Do try to be reasonably accurate in judging the amounts when buying your meat or fish. Anything that's been left outside waiting to be cooked, and which doesn't get used, will have to be binned. Salads, breads and side dishes can go back into the fridge for the next meal so you can go to town on these. New potatoes are perfect as an accompaniment and have the advantage of being delicious both hot with butter and great with mayonnaise and chives when they have cooled down. And if you know that there will be vegetarians, why not buy a small 'throwaway' barbecue on which to prepare vegetable kebabs or veggie burgers?

For more ideas on lighting the garden see IDEA 21, *An illuminating idea*, on lighting your party, and check out IDEA 27, *Make mine a double*, for a guide to estimating the quantity of alcohol you'll need.

Try another idea...

'Give a man a fish and he will eat for a day. Teach a man to fish and he will eat for a lifetime. Teach a man to create an artificial shortage of fish and he will eat steak.'
JAY LENO, comedian

Defining idea...

DRINK

Do remember that you need to provide soft drinks for the drivers – and also bear in mind that whoever is in charge of the barbecue should remain sober for safety reasons!

LIGHTING

Whether you have fully functioning exterior lights or simply rely on garden flares stuffed into terracotta pots filled with sand – which can double up as ashtrays so you don't have a garden full of butts in the morning – doesn't matter, but you do need something. If the barbie is swinging you want to be able to linger outside long into the night. A 'pub style' garden heater provides warmth and a soft glow, and is now relatively inexpensive.

Be ready to put in preparation time before your barbecue starts and it will be a sure-fire success.

Q **I understand the point of having a 'real' charcoal barbecue, but can you give me some guidelines on when to start cooking?**

How did it go?

A *Once you've lit your coals, leave them for a good half hour. Most barbecue food is ruined because chefs don't wait until the coals are ready and start to cook at a temperature that is way too high – wait until the glowing red has dimmed. The charcoal should be covered with a light white/grey ash and there should be no flames licking up the sides of the kettle or base.*

Q **Got that, so what do I do when fat or sauce drips on the coals and I get flames jumping up?**

A *Well done, you've obviously bought very juicy, good quality meat or have taken the time to marinade a dish. The solution here is to keep a trigger spray filled with water by the grill (you'll find them in your nearest garden centre). Simply give the errant flame a quick spray to quell its excesses – but don't drench the coals. You can reduce the chances of this happening by trimming any excess fat from meat beforehand.*

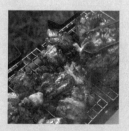 

2

In full bloom

Here are some professional secrets for choosing and arranging a perfect display of fantastic flowers.

People pay vast amounts of money to buy glamorous, professionally designed flower arrangements — but you can save yourself a fortune if you start to design your own.

Of course, it isn't just about money. If you want to impress your guests you may feel that you need a table centrepiece that is designed along quite dramatic lines. And if you have no idea how to put together such a thing then a trip to the florist is the easiest solution. But just stop and think for a minute. Flowers are essentially beautiful in their own right so it really doesn't take much practice before you can start to put together your own designer displays. Also, sometimes, the simplest ideas create the most impact.

Flower arranging can be funky; it's changed a lot since big, formal arrangements were all the rage. I've watched the world-renowned florist Jane Packer put together an amazing arrangement with the simplest of ingredients: nine gerbera, three tins of Italian tomatoes (yes, really: emptied of their contents and washed out, of course) and some natural raffia. The tins were chosen for their bright packaging, which

Here's an idea for you... **Paula Pryke is another florist who will inspire you; check out her website: www.paula-pryke-flowers.com. She also shows how you can combine unusual items in your displays – for example, an amaryllis is teamed with pebbles, roses are combined with a cabbage and germini and berries are arranged in a vase lined with lemon slices.**

provided a colourful contrast with the gerbera heads. Grouping the stems in each tin, she tied the whole group together with the raffia in a big bow about half way up the tins – it looked amazing, took virtually no time at all and, best of all, it didn't cost a fortune. People travel from all over the world to be taught at Jane's schools in London, Japan and New York – where it's based on the Upper East Side in the Terence Conran store. This is really handy – you can shop for designer vases at the same time as picking up your flower arranging skills!

Now such a quirky idea as Jane's tomato tins won't work for formal dinner parties, but why not adapt it? Take three slim vases, put a single lily in each one and run a rope of faux pearls around the three containers. See, it doesn't take much imagination to make a great display.

Defining idea...

'Flowers are the sweetest things God ever made and forgot to put a soul into.'
HENRY WARD BEECHER,
US clergyman and brother of
Harriet Beecher Stowe

Whatever the event you are planning, try to buy your flowers the day before you are going to arrange them. Put them in a bucket or container with warm water and leave them overnight. The same applies if you are going to use blooms cut from your garden.

When you come to arrange them bear in mind that you don't need to stick to flowers:

- Introduce a stem of chillies or fill the base of your vase with pebbles.
- Use coloured beads or glass cocktail stirrers.
- Include coloured plastic ice cubes or shapes – pink elephants would be fun for a birthday party piece.

Have a clean vase ready for when you start – and always use flower food in order to prolong the life of your arrangement. Most people don't realise the critical importance of preventing air from getting up the stem of the flower (this is why they can wilt very quickly) and also of removing foliage from beneath the water line. You need to do that to help discourage the growth of bacteria. So, when you start work, cut the flowers you are using under the water to prevent air from getting up the stems. Make an angled cut and strip any excess leaves or stems from them, then place in your vase or container. Carry on until all your flowers are in place.

Cut your flowers with care, use your imagination to plan the arrangement – and it will last until long after the party hangover has cleared.

Try another idea...

Flowers can be quite expensive, especially if you go mad – and it's very tempting – so have a look at IDEA 34, *The price is right*, on how to budget for the cost of events.

Defining idea...

'Arranging a bowl of flowers in the morning can give a sense of quiet in a crowded day – like writing a poem, or saying a prayer.'
ANNE MORROW LINDBERGH, the first licensed woman glider pilot in the US and wife of Charles A. Lindbergh

How did it go?

Q **I followed all your advice on cutting but the arrangement still didn't last a week. Where did I go wrong?**

A *It might be that you didn't do anything wrong. Flowers react to their environment, so consider where you put the display as this may have had an effect on the blooms. You need to avoid drastic temperature changes so keep arrangements away from windows that benefit from bright sunshine during the day. At night, make sure that they are not beside radiators or heaters and at any time of day keep them out of draughts.*

Q **OK, I've got that but my tulips are still very droopy, what can you suggest?**

A *I really love tulips, and for me their droopiness is part of their appeal. However if you want to keep them on the straight and narrow, try this: when you have your bundle of tulips, gather them up and roll them in a tight bundle of newspaper. Secure this at the top, middle and bottom with tape or an elastic band and leave them in warm water overnight.*

3

Life is a picnic

Easy essentials for entertaining at the beach or in the country. Forget about squashed pies and sand-filled sandwiches (although that gritty texture brings a certain something to the meal).

When you are going to make the effort to travel to a beautiful location for the day, don't let sloppy catering and a lack of comfort spoil the outing!

If preparation is the key to managing any event, you can multiply that ten-fold when considering a trip into the country or a day out at the seaside. Spontaneity is all well and good, but planning a trip properly will reap dividends and can ensure that it will be a day to remember.

In an ideal world, I'd have a fully equipped VW camper van. There's a romance to these vehicles that a knackered old Volvo just can't rival (much as I love the practicality of my estate car when it comes to moving furniture or ferrying dogs to the park). Just think of the joy of pulling up at the beach, folding out the canopy and settling down to lunch cooked in a fully equipped 'RV' – comfy seats are on

Here's an idea for you... **If you are intent on making up the food before you go, avoid putting tomatoes in pre-prepared sandwiches; they rarely add to the flavour when all of the pulp has soaked into the bread. Also, as you come to wrap up the bread, use greaseproof paper instead of plastic film or foil. This is slightly sturdier and will help to prevent the sandwiches from getting mushed out of shape.**

hand and even a bed if you like a late afternoon snooze. However these collector's items don't come cheap so let's return to reality and deal with picnics in the real world.

Right: there is no reason why you can't sit in comfort.

Buy a decorator's plastic sheet. This heavy-duty waterproof layer goes underneath your rugs, throws or well-worn towels. Next, make sure that you have plenty of the afore-mentioned rugs, throws or towels. There is nothing worse than settling down into a spot and realising, once everyone is seated, that someone in the group has to rest half a buttock on the rug and half on the sand or grass. Also take plenty of cushions with you. The availability of covered, machine-washable beanbags means there is no reason not to take a couple with you on your outing. Director's chairs fold up easily, so why not invest in a pair to take with you on outings to the countryside or beach?

And there is no excuse for having second-rate food, so here's some food for thought.

Defining idea... **'Tea to the English is really a picnic indoors.'**
ALICE WALKER

Soggy sandwiches in Tupperware containers are (or should be) a thing of the past. That's no criticism of Tupperware, but more an observation on what goes inside the receptacles. Sandwiches wrapped in plastic film can be potentially limp and unappetising, so think about alternatives. Why not, instead of making up the sandwiches in advance, prepare all the elements and take them in separate containers so that you can assemble them on the spot? Prepare a container filled with sliced tomatoes, another of cucumber and another of leaves. Take a pot of hummus or pre-sliced ham or roast beef. By all means butter the bread or rolls before you go (that solves the problem of butter melting in the sun) and then allow everyone to make up their own selection when they get hungry.

For the complete entertaining kit see IDEA 42, *Tools of the trade.*

Try another idea...

Of course all of this food needs to be transported to the venue and for this I would strongly recommend investing in an old fashioned shopping trolley on wheels. These are the perfect size for carrying cool boxes, bottles of drink and other assorted elements.

Keeping food fresh can be a problem, but you don't have to worry if you haven't got ice blocks. Instead fill plastic milk bottles with water and freeze overnight; only fill them two-thirds full, so that they don't burst as they freeze. They'll do the job but also, as they defrost, will give you water to wash mucky hands or rinse off plates and cutlery. (Just as an aside, there is nothing worse than struggling with plastic cutlery. Why not invest in a cheap set of knives, forks and spoons that are kept just for outings?)

'Skill without imagination is craftsmanship and gives us many useful objects such as wickerwork picnic baskets. Imagination without skill gives us modern art.'
TOM STOPPARD

Defining idea...

13

How did it go?

Q   I worked out the savoury options for the picnic but what about the sweet stuff?

A   *Well, despite ice blocks or frozen milk bottles, ice cream is clearly not an option and the chances of anything chocolatey retaining its shape is negligible. One of the best solutions I've discovered is to invest in a couple of cheesecakes from the frozen desserts cabinet at the supermarket. These can take anything from two to four hours to defrost (depending on the size and topping) so they are usually ready to eat just as you settle down for lunch.*

Q   Right, I'll give that a try. Now what do I do with the leftovers and how about some tips on clearing up?

A   *Never, ever, ever bother to take food home from a picnic. Whether it's been kept beside your iced water or not, chances are that it will have been exposed to the sun and it's just not worth recycling bits and pieces that may not be fresh. As far as clearing up is concerned, two large bin bags are usually sufficient to hold all the rubbish from a group of six. Grab a stone and drop it in the bottom of a bag when you arrive and place it near to your seating area (the stone will prevent it blowing away). Let everyone know it's there and encourage people to tidy as they go. If you have taken my advice about real cutlery, then rinse off the worst of the food with your (now melted) water, wrap the cutlery in wet paper towels and put it in a plastic bag. This will make it easier to clean once you get home.*

4

Can you hear me at the back?

Speak up and keep it clean: how to plan a speech and please your audience.

There are many reasons why I am glad to be a girl, but near the top of the list is the fact that I will never have to give a best man's speech.

I have seen friends, who were initially delighted with the honour of being asked to fulfil this role, quake and tremble on the day of the event. Of course, that's after weeks of increasingly panicky phone calls asking for any amusing stories about the groom. (Best men: these do not have to involve sexual perversions.) Now, that's not to say that I haven't had to give other speeches, I have. But somehow addressing the hockey team before a big game or work colleagues at a scheduled event isn't the same terrifying prospect.

Here's an idea for you... **Write your speech on your computer and use a large, bold font for the opening and closing sentence of each anecdote or part of the speech. This will help them to stick in your mind and guide you through the speech. Alternatively break it down and stick it on to numbered index cards, though these can be fiddly if you're nervous.**

Now, you may be called upon to be a best man, you may have to address your own family at a big birthday bash or anniversary event, or it may be a corporate party that requires your spoken contribution – but whatever the event, there are some simple guidelines that will help make the job easier.

THE WRITE STUFF

Think about these points as you write your speech:

- Make sure you consider the audience that you are writing for. A speech at a party attended by extended family that you haven't seen in years, many of whom are elderly, calls for a different tone than one which is to be delivered to work colleagues at the annual Christmas bash.
- Be clear about how long you are going to speak for and confirm this with whoever has asked you to make a speech – there is a huge difference between a five-minute and a twenty-minute welcome.
- Try to write as you would speak. Imagine that you are engaging in a conversation, which will make you seem approachable, rather than giving a lecture, which will turn people off.
- Start your speech with an ear-catching comment or dramatic statement – grab the audience's attention from the start.
- Make references to the event and the people involved two or three times in the course of your speech.
- Be humorous (run any jokes past a cynical friend beforehand just to make sure that you come across as 'funny ha ha' and not 'funny sad').

Thanks for buying one of our books! If you'd like to be placed on our mailing list to receive more information on forthcoming releases in the **52 Brilliant Ideas** series just send an e-mail to *info@infideas.com* with your name and address or simply fill in the details below and pop this card in the post. No postage is needed. We promise we won't do silly things like bombard you with lots of junk mail, nor would we even consider letting third parties look at your details. Ever.

Name:...

Address:...

....

e-mail:...

Which book did you purchase?.................................

....

Tell us what you thought of this book and our series; check out the 'Brilliant Communication' bit on the other side of this card.

I am interested in the following subjects:

☐ Health & relationships
☐ Lifestyle & leisure
☐ Arts, literature and music

☐ Careers, finance & personal development
☐ Sports, hobbies & games
☐ Actually, I'd be quite interested in:......................................

And just to say thanks, every month we'll pick 3 random names from a hat (ok, it may be some other cylindrical device) and send a complimentary book from the series. It could be you. So please tell us what book you'd like:...(check out www.52brilliantideas.com for a full list of our titles, or if you prefer we can choose one for you based on your subject interest).

You can change your life with brilliant ideas.

We're passionate about the effect our books have and we have designed them so that they can become an inspiring part of your daily routine. Our books help people to grow, giving them the confidence to believe in themselves and to transform their lives. Every day, around the world, people are regaining control of their lives with our brilliant ideas.

infiniteideas

www.52brilliantideas.com

BY AIR MAIL
par avion

Royal Mail

IBRS/CCRI NUMBER:
PHQ-D/9423/OX

NE PAS AFFRANCHIR

NO STAMP REQUIRED

RESPONSE PAYEE
GRANDE-BRETAGNE

Infinite Ideas Ltd
36 St Giles
OXFORD
GREAT BRITAIN
OX1 3LD

Brilliant Communication

- If you enjoyed this book and find yourself cuddling it at night, please tell us. If you think this book isn't fit to use as kindling, please let us know. We value your thoughts and need your honest feedback. We know if we listen to you we'll get it right. Why not send us an e-mail at *listeners@infideas.com*.

- Do you have a brilliant idea of your own that our author has missed? E-mail us at *yourauthor missedatrick@infideas.com* and if it makes it into print in a future edition or appears on our web site we'll send you four books of your choice OR the cash equivalent. You'll be fully credited (if you want) so that everyone knows you've had a brilliant idea.

- Finally, if you've enjoyed one of our books why not become an **Infinite Ideas Ambassador**. Simply e-mail ten of your friends enlightening them about the virtues of the **52 Brilliant Ideas** series and dishing out our web address: www.52brilliantideas.com. Make sure you copy us in at *ambassador@infideas.com*. We promise we won't contact them unless they contact us, but we'll send you a free book of your choice for every ten friends you email. Help spread the word!

- Involve the audience. You can ask someone a direct question – that will scare them into paying attention – throw out rhetorical questions or ask for a show of hands. (Best men, please note: 'How many people here have slept with the bride?' is not acceptable.)

As a speaker you may also be called upon to make a toast: see IDEA 36, 'Here's looking at you, kid...'

Try another idea...

Once you have run up a draft of your speech, leave it for a day and then go back to it and re-read it. Be prepared to go back and revise it two or three times before the big day.

STAND AND DELIVER

It's half an hour before you go on and you are sick with fear. There are two or three things that will help settle you and a large whisky isn't one of them; however boring it may be to stay sober at a party until your job is done, I would advise this course of action. You can make a complete idiot of yourself if you try to deliver a pre-prepared speech drunk, as chances are you will forget what you have written down or deliver it in the wrong order. So:

- Go to the toilet.
- Check your appearance.
- Brush your teeth or gargle with mouthwash.
- Make sure you have a glass of water to hand.
- Take a few good deep breaths...

'The flowery style is not unsuitable to public speeches or addresses, which amount only to compliment. The lighter beauties are in their place when there is nothing more solid to say; but the flowery style ought to be banished from a pleading, a sermon or a didactic work.'
VOLTAIRE

Defining idea...

And when you come to speak:

- Look confident – if you slouch your delivery will be poor and you'll be talking to the floor. Put your shoulders back; in that position your chest is 'open'. This will help you project your voice to the far corners of the room.
- Make eye contact – smile at people as you deliver your witty one-liners.
- Use hand gestures to help illustrate words or phrases.
- Remember to project: that's not shouting, just speaking out clearly.

Plan your speech and put in some practice hours and you'll be in demand on the 'after dinner' circuit before you know it.

Q **Well, the speech is written but I am worried about my delivery. Can you help?**

How did
it go?

A *You need to practise in front of a mirror. Remember when you had to learn how to dance and spent hours working out your moves so that you didn't look like you were insane? Now you need to be confident about how you look while speaking. As you talk to the mirror, experiment with using your hands and make sure that you are looking ahead and not at the floor. Get comfortable with glancing down at your notes for prompts then back up at the mirror without losing the flow of your speech.*

Q **OK, but I can only see my head in bathroom mirror. Now what?**

A *Get a DVD recorder and set it up to record yourself. That way you can also show the results to (carefully) selected friends or family and take on board any (positive) criticism or comments that they have about either the content of your speech or your style of delivery.*

19

5

Excuses, excuses...

Saying 'no' can be a sensitive issue. Here's a guide to the politics of telling someone you can't make it.

Let's be honest, we've all had occasions when we need to call on our creative abilities to come up with a convincing excuse for getting out of something.

It might be the neighbours' traditional Christmas Day drinks which always seem to degenerate into an awkward situation. You know the one, where the host and hostess consume too much alcohol and end up rowing loudly in the kitchen – or worse, in front of everyone else in the lounge. Or it might be the office's annual family sports day. Such occasions are usually a chance for the office hierarchy to be replicated in the hierarchy of the playing children. These are quite simply occasions where any excuse should be good enough to get you out of the event.

There is a huge difference between sending a formal note or RSVP excusing yourself from something and actually having to break the 'bad' news face to face. Whether you do have a legitimate reason for missing the event, or whether you are coming up with a reason not to attend, if you are going to tell someone face to face then I

Here's an idea for you…

Well, in fact it's more of *not* an idea. While modern technology means we are comfortable with communicating by email and text message, these are not acceptable mediums for excusing yourself at the last minute. Sending a text message, in particular, smacks of someone who is lying through their teeth and is just too scared to have a one-to-one conversation. Bite the bullet and make sure that you speak to your host.

suggest that you rehearse in front of a member of your family. They will know you well enough to point out the obvious eye twitch or scratching of the ear when you are telling a big fat fib. Body language is one thing that could give you away – or, conversely, make you appear genuine – while if you were on the phone you wouldn't have to worry about a thing. When we lie our subconscious knows it and as a consequence acts independently from the rest of us, sending out nervous energy that can translate into twitches or gestures which give the game away. A classic example of this is not being able to look the other person in the eye. I've tried to conquer this one by staring my boyfriend in the eye when I reassure him that I've only had a couple of drinks and am swaying from tiredness not drunkenness. Unfortunately he has now learnt that if I maintain eye contact for any length of time I am probably trying to pull a fast one.

Anyway, if you have a cast-iron reason not to attend, you have nothing to worry about.

Defining idea…

'No one lies so boldly as the man who is indignant.'
FRIEDRICH NIETZSCHE

However, if you aren't prone to lying your way out of engagements, you might want to be aware of the following when planning your excuse:

- Short and snappy is better than long and convoluted, though a few specific details will give the excuse a realistic feel.
- Staying as close to the truth as possible always helps to reduce the chance of being caught out.
- If you have avoided the same social occasion repeatedly, you might be better off doing it once just to get it out of the way.

By far the easiest way to excuse yourself from any event is by sending a letter or note; if you have received a formal invite this makes it all the easier. You'll probably be given a date by which time you are expected to RSVP. RSVP comes from *répondez s'il vous plaît*, and means that whoever sent the invite wants to know whether you are going to be there or not. Please don't just ignore this; it is there because people need to know one or more of these things: who to sit at particular tables, how much drink or food to order, how many glasses/chairs/tables to hire. By not responding (whether you are attending or not) you are making the host's life difficult, so get on the case as quickly as possible. Choose from two options to start your note: 'I regret that I am unable to attend...' or 'Unfortunately, I will not be able to attend...'. Either one is an acceptable form.

OK, now, don't delay and start on your excuses today.

So you didn't want to go to a party where you thought you wouldn't know a soul. See IDEA 35, *All by myself*, for some help.

Try another idea...

'It is a good rule in life never to apologize. The right sort of people do not want apologies, and the wrong sort take a mean advantage of them.'
P.G. WODEHOUSE

Defining idea...

23

How did it go?

Q   Well, I originally said I was going to the party but now I'm too tired to leave the house. Will they miss me?

A   *That is so lame. Unless there has been a major accident, serious family health problem or you are being held hostage by the boss in a meeting, then you really should drag your sorry arse into the shower, have a fluff up and get out to the party. Look, even if you only stay for an hour, at least you have made the effort. Just one thing. Don't sneak out hoping no one will spot you. It is very bad etiquette to leave without saying goodbye and thanking your host or hostess.*

Q   No, I mean it. I really am suffering from exhaustion – I am off to the doctor's first thing in the morning. Now can I stay at home?

A   *Forgive my cynicism. In this case, you have got to get on the phone and let your host know the situation. Then after you've been to the doctor make sure that you send a small gift with a note of apology – a bottle of wine or small bouquet is sufficient and will ensure that you aren't crossed off the Christmas card list.*

6
Young at heart

Throwing perfect parties for children can be really complicated, so here are some suggestions to make them run smoothly.

Kids expect more than a game of Pass the Parcel and a party dress these days.

I'm talking about events for children who still require adult supervision. Some parents might suggest that this is the case even at an eighteenth birthday bash, but I am thinking more of children of about six to twelve. Dealing with this younger age group, I don't need to get into the rights and wrongs of alcohol or the possibility of a sneaky joint being passed around...

I will come clean at this point and tell you that I don't have kids of my own so I have never had sole responsibility for hosting my own children's parties, but there have been plenty of occasions when I have been roped in. When I was little the prospect of playing Pin the Tail on the Donkey or Musical Bumps was enough to guarantee that I'd have my hands washed and my party frock on in plenty of time. Maybe I'm being cynical about this, but today children have much higher expectations of what a party should offer.

Here's an idea for you... **If you're hosting the party at a venue, check and see if they can offer you somewhere to store presents. When you are trying to ferry children around and keep to a specific timetable you may not have space in the car or time at the event to gather together all the gifts and get them home. If the venue can supply a safe storage space, you can return and retrieve them once everyone is home safely.**

There are two options. Pick a location where you can take the children for their special day or put in some extra effort to host the event at home. Here's a simple list of what you may need to consider whatever you decide:

- Numbers – how many children can you accommodate and how many adults can you drag in to help out?
- Invitations – shop-bought invites featuring favourite cartoon or TV characters will appeal to your child.
- The cake – consider how many slices you will need to get out of this. A tray bake is much easier to cut into a specific number.
- Decorations – how much are you going to dress up your home, or if you are using a venue can you leave this up to them?
- Food – sandwiches and plenty of crisps used to satisfy me, but pizza is a possibility for today's more demanding youngsters and can be fine for small vegetarians without the others feeling deprived.
- Games or activities – are you going to hire an entertainer or make up your games? Do you want to have a mini-disco (in which case a couple of chart-topping compilation discs are a must)?
- Party bags – as any child will tell you, these are how the party will be judged, so budget for some exciting treats for the guests to take away.

The budget is up to you. Bear in mind that it may be better to invite fewer children and bring in an entertainer, so that you can afford something really special, rather than have loads of kids and find that you have very little money

Try and get the thank-you letters written as quickly as possible after receiving gifts. See IDEA 12, *I'm much obliged.*

Try another idea...

left over once the essentials have been taken care of. One piece of advice when the birthday child is very young – keep the numbers down; too many people and too much excitement can lead to tears. Don't forget, that if parents are going to stay at the party (and when children are small this is the best way to ensure things run as smoothly as possible) you may want to include some wine for them on your shopping list.

If you decide to have the party away from your home you'll need to ask some questions about the facilities and party packages on offer. The earlier that you get this organised, the better. There are a few points that should be up for discussion:

- Is there a defined area for your group or are you just another table on the day?
- What is the price per head? Don't be afraid to negotiate on this and remember there may be adults who need to be catered for.
- Do you have to leave by a particular time?
- Where are the toilet facilities?
- What sort of activities can they provide; how are they supervised?
- Are there any specific safety requirements?

'The essence of childhood, of course, is play.'
BILL COSBY

Defining idea...

A children's party is potentially a stressful affair, so take the worry out of the occasion by getting everything in place and you too can enjoy yourself.

How did
it go?

Q **I've followed your advice on planning a party at home and I can tick everything on the checklist but I'd like to have a rough timetable for the event. Any tips?**

A *This depends on the age of the children because the younger they are, the shorter their attention span. They'll already be very excited when they arrive, so consider having a reasonably quiet activity to kick things off; after twenty minutes or so you can engage them in something more active. Following two or three lively games it may be time to sit down for the party food. Set aside some time after the food has been eaten for presents to be opened but don't drag this out. It can be difficult when young children see someone else opening lots of gifts without receiving anything themselves, so engage them all in a game where each participant can find a gift.*

Q **What do I do if someone throws a tantrum?**

A *In a group of over-excited children there is always the potential for someone to get upset. Take the child aside and give them the chance to calm down; you must also allow them to vent their feelings. If the cause was someone else behaving badly towards them, then they need you to understand their frustration and, if appropriate, sympathise with their position. Finding something to divert their attention may help to diffuse the situation completely.*

7

Lifelong love affair

Anniversaries should be a cause for great celebration.

Let's be brutally frank about this. These days, the longer a couple stays together, the more miraculous it seems. And you don't have to be married to celebrate it!

I am delighted when I hear of people who have stayed married for five, ten or twenty years. I make every effort to send cards to friends and family members on their anniversaries because I truly believe people should be lauded and applauded for making a marriage work. I know there are plenty of couples who don't feel the need to formalise their relationship with a marriage certificate. If that's you please don't just turn the page – there's no reason why you can't celebrate exactly the same milestones even if you aren't wearing a wedding ring. And anyone can end up having to organise an anniversary party for someone else.

Now, in the early years of the relationship, gifts can be pretty easily (and inexpensively) given. It's only when you have put in a good few years' service that the traditional themes get more and more expensive, as you will see from the following list.

Here's an idea for you...

Tradition says that the top layer of a wedding cake is kept to be eaten on the first anniversary. While you will have thanked all of your ushers, bridesmaids, parents, whoever on the day of your marriage, why not send them a thank-you note a year on? It's a lovely gesture to send a piece of cake – you can buy cake boxes to send through the post – with the note.

1st: paper
2nd: cotton
3rd: leather
4th: fruit and flower; linen
5th: wood
6th: sugar and sweets; iron
7th: wool; copper
8th: bronze and rubber (yes, really)
9th: pottery and willow
10th: tin; aluminium
11th: steel
12th: silk and fine linen
13th: lace
14th: ivory
15th: crystal, and then...
20th: china
25th: silver
30th: pearls; ivory
35th: coral; jade
40th: rubies
45th: sapphires
50th: gold
55th: emeralds
60th: diamonds

In the early years, an anniversary is very much an occasion on which gifts are given between the couple. After all, everyone who came to your wedding gave you a gift on that day, so it would be more than greedy to expect something every year after that.

Family events can bring with them a certain amount of stress. See IDEA 51, *Family fun*, for some tips on coping with family gatherings.

Try another idea...

Do put in the effort with your partner to mark the occasion. I would make a point of putting the date on the kitchen calendar. That way you won't have that stomach-churning feeling when you produce a card and gift on the day and your other half has completely forgotten. They then have to run out to the shops at the last minute, which always takes the gloss off any subsequent declarations of love. Especially if all that's open is the local petrol station.

FAMILY AFFAIRS

It's really only when you start to get to the big numbers that it's appropriate to go to town with friends or family by inviting people to an event. From a twentieth anniversary onwards, there is a strong possibility that it will fall to the couple's children to arrange a party.

'What ought to be done to the man who invented the celebrating of anniversaries? Mere killing would be too light.'
MARK TWAIN

Defining idea...

31

While you may want to plan it as a surprise, there is a case for making the couple aware that something is being planned. One reason for this is that you can then arrange for a special gift by asking guests to donate money in advance. You could use this to pay for a weekend away or a particular piece of furniture. If you know that your parents have had the same set of china for years, supplemented by mismatched bits and pieces acquired over time, it could be appropriate to buy them a complete set for their twentieth – china – anniversary. While frivolous gifts are a delight, sometimes the better option is practical rather than pretty, something that the recipients need and will use. And if you're going to approach guests for money then you must speak to them by telephone or in person. Make sure that you explain to them why you are hosting the event and your reasoning for the gift idea. It is unthinkable to send out a postal invitation with a request for money.

At the party, try some of these ideas. Buy a large card, big enough for everyone who is attending the event to sign. That way your parents will have record of everyone who has contributed to the gift. Now, place a camera beside the card and take a picture of everyone as they sign, so that there will be a visual record of those who attended the party. As anyone who has hosted any kind of event will testify, the hours can fly by; it's a great idea to have photos that you can refer to the next day. The recipients will want to send out thank-you letters, and this is one way of making sure that everyone who contributed to the gift receives a note. Do wait until everyone has arrived and had time to chat before presenting the gift; if you are having a sit-down dinner or buffet then wait until coffee has been served before making the presentation.

Q **I forgot our last anniversary so I want to make this one something special. It'll be our fifth, which according to you is marked by wood. This doesn't seem very romantic, any ideas?**

How did it go?

A *You're right. In all honesty, you need to think laterally: consider a weekend away to a particularly beautiful part of the country where you can walk in a forest. Or why not take a cruise or go out on a wooden boat for a day?*

Q **Sounds lovely, but I am working to a budget here... What else can you suggest?**

A *I'll bet if you search local restaurants, you can find somewhere that has a wood-panelled dining room, or an open log fire. Alternatively cook something at home and serve up an oaky Chardonnay.*

8

The cocktail-hour kit

When you want to serve up stylish drinks, the right cocktail makes the ultimate place to start. But you do need some kit.

Everyone has a 'perfect cocktail' story. Whether it was the location, the company, the drink, or the dreamy barman...

That was the moment when everything came together and you sipped your favourite tipple and longed for it to last all night. I was in New York, taking a trip with a girlfriend. We looked in the guide books for cool places to drink and ended up in one. The lighting was dark and the tables were pretty full, but we found a corner and sat down and ordered. I had a Vodka Martini, and I can't remember a more sublime first sip.

It's important to hold on to that feeling when you decide to start mixing drinks for yourself. Because the person that served your perfect drink is no different from you – except they had the equipment to do the job properly. They also used the best ingredients. Now, any barman worth his salt should be able to make a mix of cocktails. While bar staff might have learnt all the right techniques, as much as anything it's those right ingredients and having the right equipment that mean they can deliver what you want. So, if you can fulfil those two criteria then you too can deliver the same result in the comfort of your own home.

Here's an idea for you... **Why not consider attending a bar school to get a good grounding? Look for a one-day course that will combine an introduction to the world of cocktails with a practical foundation in the mechanics of cocktail preparation. Check that you will cover some of the following techniques which will stand you in good stead when you start to make your drinks at home: building a drink, muddling, layering, straining and smashing... sounds like fun!**

Let's look at the essential tools here.

You wouldn't expect to be able to make a delicious dinner without having sharp knives, mixing bowls, easy-to-use peelers and versatile dishes to help you prepare the food properly. So don't think you can mix up designer drinks without the requisite tools of the trade. There's a pretty long list of what you could buy, but for starters let's consider the basic things.

Cocktail shaker. This has two purposes. Firstly, it allows you to mix the ingredients; secondly, with the addition of ice, it allows you to chill the drink. There are two different types. The first is made up of three metal components: tumbler, strainer and lid. The second has just two parts, a metal tumbler and glass tumbler. If you opt for the latter you will also need a strainer. Many professionals believe it is better to use a two-part shaker with a separate strainer, as it is quicker to pour the drink.

Jigger. This is a double-sided measuring device with a small cup at each end. It's used so that you can get the amounts in your drinks correct. When you're cooking you need to measure all the ingredients in the dish correctly; the same applies to your cocktails. It is important to combine the right amounts, as even the smallest error will affect the taste. The larger measure is usually one and a half ounces; the smaller side is an ounce. A good jigger will allow you to pour the spirit cleanly into the glass.

Look at drinks in **IDEA 9**, *Stocking up*, **to work out what you will need.**

Try another idea...

Strainer. The Hawthorn strainer is recognisable by the wire spring that runs around the edge of the rim. This prevents ice cubes from falling into the drink but allows any fruit pulp to drip through. The Julep strainer looks like a little colander and takes a lot more practice to use properly.

Bar spoon. Essential for making certain cocktails that need to be stirred not shaken – apologies to 007.

Juicer. You can pinch the one from the kitchen as long as it is quick and easy to use.

Muddler. A device used to muddle or mash ingredients such as mint leaves or lime quarters in order to release their oils or flavours.

Those are the main items. You might also want to think about some swizzle sticks, a cutting board and knife, an ice crusher and a martini pitcher. Remember also that in order for your drinks to look the part you will need to invest in some stylish glasses.

Now, there are a plethora of other items that you will acquire as you learn more about making cocktails, but get used to working with these as your starting point and you'll be mixing delicious drinks in minutes.

'I have taken more out of alcohol than alcohol has taken out of me.'
WINSTON CHURCHILL

Defining idea...

37

Q   I have a clear idea on most of the items I need to buy but what do I look for in a 'muddler'?

A   *Right, as I have said, this is used to mash ingredients to get the flavour out of them. If you think about the grinding that you do when using a pestle and mortar you will get an idea of what you are going to be doing. They all look pretty much the same – like tiny wooden baseball bats or like a wooden pestle without the need for the mortar.*

Q   I really don't like bits in my drinks; is it essential?

A   *That depends on how fashionable your friends are because the current vogue for Caipirinhas means you will need to muddle. If you don't invest in one you won't be able to offer anyone a Mint Julep either, which would be a shame as this is one classic cocktail that everyone should try at least once in their lives.*

9

Stocking up

Invest in a few different spirits in order to get your cocktail bar up and running. So how many different kinds of spirits do you need?

Reverting to clichés, how long is a piece of string?

If you walk into any shop dedicated to selling drink, the sheer number and variety of bottles is astonishing. What you don't want to do is attempt to mimic the shelves in your local bar. It would cost you a fortune.

You have two choices. Option one is to find a really good cocktail bar and visit it two or three times, trying a couple of drinks on each occasion. I am not advocating that you get falling-down drunk. Just use the visits to decide on your favourite three or four cocktails. Alternatively, the cheaper option, option two, is to pick up a cocktail book and go through the list, again selecting the cocktails that you like. Try and make sure that the ingredients differ. Here are some of the options available to you:

- Brandy cocktails: Brandy Alexander, Sidecar, Stinger, Between the Sheets.
- Gin cocktails: Gibson, Gin Fizz, Gimlet, Singapore Sling.
- Rum cocktails: Rum Punch, Jolly Roger, Dark Daiquiri, Jamaican Mule.
- Vodka cocktails: Seabreeze, Woo Woo, Cosmopolitan, Metropolitan.
- Bourbon cocktails: Mint Julep, Old Fashioned, Boston Sour, Kentucky Derby.
- Tequila cocktails: Margarita, Tequini, Freddy Fuddpucker, Shady Lady.
- Vermouth cocktails: Manhattan, Negroni, Rob Roy, Americano…

Choose one gin-based cocktail, one that's vodka based, one with vermouth and one that is made with bourbon. Or you might favour light or dark rum, tequila or brandy.

Just as an example, here are four that I favour:
- Black Russian, which contains vodka and coffee liqueur.
- Daiquiri, which contains light rum, lime juice and sugar syrup.
- Martini, which contains gin or vodka and vermouth.
- Tequila Sunrise, which contains tequila, lime juice, orange juice and grenadine.

Whether you have followed option one or two above (the bar or the book) you should also take note of the type of glass that your drink is served in: and no, this doesn't mean you have to sit in a cocktail bar for hours – a good cocktail book will tell you. Some will come in shapely glasses, others are served in classic tumblers or slim, tall vessels. As a guideline, strong cocktails come in smaller glasses; those with a large amount of juice or mixers that make them more of a refreshing drink are served in taller glasses. The presentation is part and parcel of creating the perfect cocktail so when you budget for your bar do figure in an investment in a range of different glasses.

Here's an idea for you...

When you are ready to try out your bartending skills, write out a cocktail menu for guests to choose from. You want to be able to offer people the drinks that you have perfected, so printing up or writing out a list will offer people a choice while keeping the options limited to your perfected mixes.

By looking at the sample list of cocktails above you'll see that in addition to the main spirit you will need to buy some additional bottles, so make a list of all the ingredients for each recipe. Now you can go shopping.

Once you have your ingredients, there are various techniques that can be used in mixing the drinks:

If you are serving lots of drinks, see IDEA 16: *Ouch, ouch, ouch...* You may need it!

Try another idea...

- Shake a drink: all of the ingredients are put into the shaker, the lid is put on and then it's shaken until the outside of the container frosts.
- Build a drink: this describes the process of pouring the ingredients straight into the glass in which it will be served. With this technique you may need a bar spoon or stirrer to blend the ingredients.
- Layer a drink: The different ingredients are poured over the back of a bar spoon into the glass in which the drink will be served. Different types of alcohol have different gravities so the heaviest goes in first and the next will, if you pour it carefully, sit on top in a separate layer.

'A lonely man is a lonesome thing, a stone, a bone, a stick, a receptacle for Gilbey's gin.'
JOHN CHEEVER, US novelist

Defining idea...

So now you can start mixing. Once you have perfected your three or four drinks, look up other cocktails that have the same ingredients and begin to experiment with these. Over time you can add to your collection of bottles and expand your range of drinks.

'The proper union of gin and vermouth is a great and sudden glory; it is one of the happiest marriages on earth, and one of the shortest lived.'
BERNARD DE VOTO, American writer

Defining idea...

How did
it go?

Q **I am perfecting the art of shaking but need to get a clearer idea of what to do with the ice. I don't always want to use cubes and sometimes I need it crushed. Any tips?**

A *I find the easiest way to crush ice is to put some cubes in a plastic bag. Wrap this in a tea towel and then use a rolling pin to smash the ice.*

Q **And what if the drink calls for shaved ice?**

A *Then you will need to invest in a special ice-shaving machine which you will be able to buy from any website that supplies cocktail kit.*

Q **More on the subject of ice, if you don't mind. One of my favourite cocktails is a Margarita; do I use ice to wet the rim of the glass before I dip it in salt?**

A *Not if you want to enjoy it. Rub the rim with a piece of lime before you dip it in the salt. If you are going to be mixing up a lot of Margaritas then I would suggest that you invest in a glass rimmer – it's a piece of cocktail kit that serves as a container for salt (or sugar, depending on the drink that you are mixing) and makes the job of dressing up your cocktails that much easier.*

10

Prepare to party

Designing a kitchen when you will be entertaining on a regular basis takes careful planning.

The combination of food preparation, presentation, drinking and dining means heavy demands will be made on the space. Get it right and life will be easier.

It's a tall order for just one room. So why not consider each activity that may take place there and put them in order of priority? If you are planning to bring in caterers for home entertaining then ample work surfaces are essential. If you will be doing all of the cooking then your priorities will be a generous fridge, an 'all singing, all dancing' cooker and cupboards arranged so that it's easy to reach serving platters and oven-to-tableware.

Here's an idea for you...

With lots of food preparation in store, well-planned waste disposal is a high priority. A small swing bin just won't cut it. The best solution is to combine a waste disposal into your sink area so that food scraps can be dealt with quickly and hygienically. Look for a large sink (a double-basin design is ideal) and fit the waste disposal unit beneath the waste outlet of the basin. Make sure that people who use the kitchen are aware of it; stray cutlery can cause havoc with a disposal unit. Also be aware that these units can be quite noisy, so if you are designing a kitchen/diner make sure that the sink is positioned well away from the dining area.

BASICS

One of the most important aspects of planning this room is to make sure that your appliances are up to the job. You need to think about the fridge, freezer, cooker and, of course, dishwasher. An all-in-one fridge-freezer for example, just won't have the capacity to hold endless prepared platters, several bottles of beautifully chilled Pouilly-Fumé, frozen deserts and essential ice cubes. Why not invest in a fridge with a built-in ice-maker so that you won't run out of cubes and buy a separate chest freezer which, if you need to save on space, can be put in the garage or utility room? You'll be a keen cook if you plan to entertain a lot, and so make sure you have – at the very least – a big double oven and a hob with at least six burners. A microwave is essential but again, if you need to save space, look for one that can be mounted on brackets under eye-level cupboards and so keep the work surface clear of clutter.

CLEAN LIVING

During the dinner or party, you don't want
your guests to look at piled-up plates and food-
encrusted cutlery so make sure that your dishwasher has room for a minimum of
two courses' worth of clutter. Buying a small one that sits on the work surface or
one that only takes a few plates just isn't enough. And if fitting all this kit into the
kitchen is causing you a headache, then go to an experienced kitchen planner and
stress the importance of these pieces in the scheme for your room. Clever kitchen
planning means a sink can be installed in a corner and a slimline fridge fitted into a
space that is too small for a standard-width kitchen cabinet.

So what else should be considered? Flexible lighting and practical flooring come to
mind. While you are preparing food you need task lighting. That means spots or
overhead lights where the beams brighten the preparation and cooking areas. A
cooker hood with built-in light offers a simple solution for the cooking area, and a
directional spot is ideal for the sink and chopping area.

Flooring needs to stay looking good even after several groups of people have
traipsed into the room to greet you, grab a drink or help clear the table. I had a
friend who put down white ceramic tiles in the kitchen because she wanted to keep
the area as light as possible – what a mistake. The floor was often filthy before her
parties had even started to get lively. Look for
flooring or tiles with tonal variations – a faux-
marble vinyl, or a travertine or sandstone
where colour variations in the surface will
disguise a multitude of sins.

See IDEA 15, *The time to dine*, on the practicalities of dinner parties.

Try another idea...

'Real pleasure goes hand in hand with practicality: a kitchen that is functional will also be a place of creative satisfaction...'
SIR TERENCE CONRAN, *Easy Living*

Defining idea...

How did it go?

Q **I have a large room and want to use part of it as a dining area but I want it to feel like a separate space. What can I do to achieve this?**

A   *If your kitchen is large enough for you to use it as a kitchen/diner then it's a good idea to try and define the two different areas when putting together your design scheme. There are two very simple ways of achieving this. The first is to use two different colours on the walls in the two areas. These can be a lighter and darker shade of the same colour, for example a pale taupe in the kitchen and a slightly darker brown in the dining area. The second way is to change the flooring in the two spaces. You can use different coloured tiles, or change the colour or type of the flooring.*

Q **I get the paint idea but won't using different flooring create a dip or ridge in the middle of the floor?**

A   *Fair point, but you can avoid this with tiles by choosing two different designs from the same collection. With a vinyl or linoleum flooring always use a skilled fitter who will ensure that the join between the two will not lift or come apart.*

11
It's in the post

There are occasions when you will want to send out a formal invitation; here's how to go about it with style.

When it comes to organised affairs such as weddings and anniversary parties, you will be sending out an invite by mail. It's worth taking the trouble to get it right.

Make some decisions early on. Think carefully; you are, even though it may be subconscious, indicating the mood of the event and you will want to consider all the following things – the colour, texture and weight of the paper (remember that the envelopes will match), the style of the type, traditional or contemporary, and the colour of the printed text.

Now you need to think about how much information you need to give and the various options that are required. A good example of this is a wedding. For example, if all the guests are invited to the ceremony and the reception, then that involves one type of invite. However, if you are having a ceremony with a small, select group and then a reception involving more people you will need two different ones. Have a clear idea of your requirements before you place an order.

Here's an idea for you...

When you are budgeting for the invitations, do remember that you need to include the cost of postage. You may want to get samples of different weights of paper and envelopes to see just how much the postage varies. If you choose a heavy card, this is clearly going to push up the cost of postage. When you consider, depending on the event, that you could be sending out 200 invitations, postage can seriously mount up.

IT'S ONLY WORDS

Make a rough draft of the information that you want to include. Remember the essentials: the date (include the day), the time (start and finish times) and the location; it's surprisingly easy to miss something important or get it wrong. If the venue is difficult or awkward to find, you'll need to give clear directions, and it's the norm to provide these in an enclosure. You may have decided on a dress code, so indicate that on your invitation. While this may seem a little dictatorial it makes sense to guide people; everyone is uncomfortable if they arrive at an event and feel that their outfit is wrong for the occasion.

It's quite likely that you will need to have an accurate idea of numbers well in advance. Whether you need to allocate places for your seating plan, or make sure that the event is not under- or over-catered, it makes sense to give people plenty of time to RSVP. Including a response card with the invite will, without a shadow of a doubt, encourage people to answer more quickly than if they have to write their own. Should you provide a stamped addressed envelope? My advice would be yes, although it will add to your overall costs.

So what should you say? Depending on the nature of the event you can follow these guidelines:

- A formal affair: *You are cordially invited...*
- A casual event: *Come and join us...*
- Celebrating the birth of your baby: *We are delighted to announce...*
- Throwing a housewarming: *Join us with friends and new neighbours...*

If you have to plan your event quickly, see IDEA 38, *At the last minute*, for some helpful hints.

Try another idea...

Once you are happy with the phrasing, ask someone who is detached from the organisation of the event to read it. They may spot an error or omission in the invite.

NOW YOU ARE READY TO PLACE YOUR ORDER...

When invites are custom-made you will be provided with a proof, but once you have given the go-ahead the invitations can't be returned. Don't forget that you can request samples before you commit yourself to a particular design, and when you get the proof make sure that it is read by a couple of people: have the relevant details written down somewhere else so that they can be cross-checked. Be sure to order enough invitations: any extras are generally charged at the same rate as a new order and most stationers recommend adding twenty-five more than you think you'll need. You might also like to have matching items at the event – menu cards or personalised napkins for the tables, perhaps.

'The only man who is really free is the one who can turn down an invitation to dinner without giving an excuse.'
JULES RENARD, French author

Defining idea...

Don't forget: from placing your order to receiving your invites can take up to four weeks. In an ideal world you want to be sending out invitations at least a couple of months before any event, so make sure that you allow plenty of time.

49

How did it go?

Q **I have drafted the information that I need to give on my wedding invite but my parents are divorced so I need to know how to phrase it. Can you help?**

A *There are accepted forms of address in this situation. Here are your options. If your mother has remarried: 'Mr James Cook and Mrs John Fraser request the pleasure of your company...' If your mother has not remarried: 'Mr James Cook and Mrs Anne Cook request the pleasure...' If your mother has remarried and is hosting the event with your stepfather: 'Mr and Mrs John Fraser request the pleasure of your company at the marriage of her daughter...'*

Q **Where should I indicate the dress code on my wedding invites?**

A *The correct place is the bottom right-hand corner.*

Q **And what about the gift list?**

A *If you are having a gift list please do not put this on the main invitation. People will usually call to find out if there is a list somewhere. If you do want to put in the details, then include them on a separate slip with the invitation.*

12

I'm much obliged

There are many occasions when it's right to say thanks.

The art of letter writing is in decline. Because it's easier to fire off an email or send a quick text, contacting people by post is the exception and not the norm.

So this makes it all the more special when you do send a hand-written missive that expresses thanks for a gift or a service performed. Not only is it good manners, it also shows that you have thought about the person concerned. The best advice I can give is to write as you speak; that way it will not sound too formal or too forced, so be chatty and relaxed. There are no rules, no formal etiquette and no right or wrong. Actually that's not true. There is one rule.

Write your thank-you letters as soon as you can!

If you put it off so that weeks pass by, you may forget your feelings and actions at the time. For example: a speech that someone made reduced you to tears; a gift that you opened was something that you had coveted for years. By writing your thank-you letter quickly, the power of the emotion that you felt at the time will translate into words and make the expression of gratitude all the more meaningful.

Here's an idea for you...

If you are writing to someone who sent a gift when invited to a christening, wedding or anniversary celebration even though they were unable to attend, then include a photograph from the event. Whether it is a group shot of everyone who was there on the day, or a close-up of the baby or the happy couple, it goes a little way towards helping them share the experience.

As I have stated, there are no rules (with that one exception) but as a guideline, consider the following approach. Firstly, decide the format. Are you going to buy a card or put pen to paper? In which case choose good quality paper and invest in matching envelopes. If you are using a shop-bought card, then make sure that you write a personal note and don't just sign under the printed message.

Now, don't fall into the trap of opening with 'I am just writing to say…'. Yes, it's an easy way in, but you are stating the obvious. Always put a service that someone performed for you in context, for example: 'Your job description was best man and you really lived up to that title on the day.' If you're acknowledging a gift, then mention it and make reference to how it has been used: 'The wine glasses are beautiful and we raise a toast to you every time we crack open a bottle.' If you have received money, then say how it is going to be spent. And thank the people you're writing to at the beginning of the letter, then thank them again at the end.

So when should you send a note and are there occasions when it isn't necessary? Again it is hard to come up with hard and fast rules but use the following situations as a guide.

When to send:

- To the host or hostess when a party has been given in your honour.
- For presents for the birth of a new baby or christening gifts.
- After you have stayed in someone's house.
- After a wedding.
- On receipt of sympathy flowers and letters.
- After being entertained by the boss.
- After receiving gifts or flowers during a hospital stay.

When to use your own discretion:

- When you have thanked people as you opened a gift in their presence.
- After a job interview.
- After being a guest at a small dinner party.
- If a friend or neighbour has helped you out with taking in the post and checking on the house while you are on holiday.
- If someone has stepped in at very short notice to babysit/dogsit.

As a final point, do try and handwrite the letter with a decent pen. Even though it is so much quicker to run something out on the computer, it lacks the personal touch and looks like a circular even if it doesn't read like one.

When you get invited to any event remember acceptable rules of behaviour. See IDEA 44, The good guest guide.

Try another idea...

'As we express our gratitude, we must never forget that the highest appreciation is not to utter words, but to live by them.'
JOHN F. KENNEDY

Defining idea...

53

Q **I've got the general idea and am drafting the wedding gift thank-you notes a day at a time. What do I say to people who sent gifts even though they couldn't make the wedding?**

A *Just approach this as any other thank-you letter. As I've already mentioned, you may want to include a picture. The wording of the letter should be along the following lines:*
'Dear Jo and Alex,
Thank you very much for the lovely linen, which we received last week. It was so considerate of you to think about us on our special day. We were so sorry that you were unable to share the time with us but trust that you will enjoy looking at the enclosed photo. We look forward to seeing you and hope it won't be long before the next party where we can meet up.'

Q **Brilliant, that gets another one nearly out of the way – just one more bit of advice, please. We very rarely see these people and don't know them very well even though they are family. How should I sign off?**

A *Well 'lots of love' would be too effusive, even if they were family. I would suggest settling for 'warm regards', 'take care' or 'with our very best wishes', and then your names. PS: Do not, under any circumstances, add any kisses!*

13

Smoke signals

Cigarettes, cigars and even pipes are part and parcel of the party scene. How do you deal with this?

The presence of smokers at any event is increasingly the cause of debate...

Should they be allowed to light up? Are they poisoning those around them? Are the hosts being too dictatorial if they decide that a 'no smoking' rule should apply?

The debate will certainly run and run and run. If you are struggling with this dilemma while considering where you are going to hold an event then there is a very simple solution – many places (listed buildings, art galleries and the like) don't allow smoking on the premises anyway, so choose somewhere which operates this policy and the decision is taken out of your hands.

The law may specify where smoking is allowed but if not, and in general terms, I don't think it is fair to smoke in spaces when non-smokers have no option but to be there – planes, trains, buses and coaches for example. However, in pubs, clubs, bars and restaurants I think it is up to the individuals concerned to work out their own rules of behaviour. If you are hosting an event at home, then it is important that you make your own smoking rules clear.

Here's an idea for you... **Copy a trick that many pubs use and invest in a firm paintbrush before your party. Use this to brush out ashtrays when you empty them. It saves having to constantly wash out ash and leaves them dry so that any cigars or cigarettes that are left burning don't get sodden tips.**

MAKING BOUNDARIES

Now, as a smoker, I always drift towards the kitchen at parties. I'd probably head in that direction anyway, as it is usually where you'll find the ice for your drink and tends to be the place where like-minded drinkers congregate. In my experience, most smokers will do the same: the kitchen often leads onto the garden, and the door can be left open to dispel the worst of the smoke. If the weather is fine, this also encourages people to smoke outside.

Make a decision about the smoking policy at your party, and do not be embarrassed to put up signs that make it clear. If it's a family affair, and babies and children will be present, then send the smokers outside. If it's an adult affair, the choice is yours but if you don't smoke then do not feel obliged to let people light up in every room. I really do stress this; it is perfectly acceptable to make it clear that smoking is only allowed in one designated space. Put out ashtrays in one area – that will give a clear message. However, if you are going to allow smoking in the house then do provide proper ashtrays and don't leave it to the smokers to drop butts into bottles or cans, which can become very messy.

Consider the following:

- Make sure that windows are open in the smoking area.
- Have scented candles to light where people will be smoking (plug-in air fresheners are hideous to look at but it might be worth buying one and positioning it in a socket where no one will be able to see it. If you do go down this road, set it on the lowest setting – the 'scent' can be seriously overpowering.
- Provide proper ashtrays.
- Clear them out regularly.

Clearing out ashtrays is a bore, but is part of the general mess that a party creates. See IDEA 19, *It's a messy business...*

Try another idea...

Now, there are rules that smokers should adhere to:

- Always ask the host if it is acceptable to smoke.
- Never light up if someone at your table is still eating.
- Ask if you can smoke if no ashtrays have been provided.
- If you are in a jazz club at midnight – you can.
- If you light a cigarette then smoke it; don't just wave it about.
- Turn your head and exhale away from the person that you are talking to.
- Extinguish it properly.
- Even if there are ashtrays on the table, the best-mannered smokers will not light up until after dessert has been served and eaten.

Of course it may be that your government has made the decision – or will do so in the future – about where and when people can smoke.

'Tobacco and alcohol, delicious fathers of abiding friendships and fertile reveries.'
LUIS BUÑUEL

Defining idea...

How did it go?

Q   I am going to put ashtrays in the kitchen at my party but how do I prevent people carrying them to other spaces and smoking there?

A   *The simplest and most effective way of controlling this is to make it completely clear to guests whom you know smoke as they arrive. Make a casual comment as you take their coats, or offer to get them a drink and simply say 'By the way, I know you'll want a smoke so I've put out ashtrays in the kitchen. I'd really appreciate it if you could smoke in there.'*

Q   But I know what they are like when they've had a drink or two! Can you suggest anything?

A   *Yes. Don't be a wimp about this, it's your home. If anyone is so ignorant that they ignore such a specific request, are you sure that you want them at your party anyway? Make one of your closest friends your partner in crime and ask them to help ensure that the smokers stick to the designated area. Remove ashtrays if they appear in other parts of the house and mention to people around why you are doing this. It's not just about the smoke, it's about the possibility of burns or scorch marks on furniture and carpets as well.*

14

Be my guest

Make it a memorable break for people who come to stay...

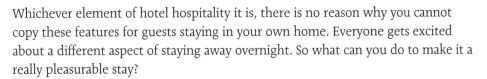

What are the best things about checking into a hotel? Is it the crisp clean sheets, the chocolate on the pillow or the assortment of mini toiletries that are provided for your personal pleasure?

Whichever element of hotel hospitality it is, there is no reason why you cannot copy these features for guests staying in your own home. Everyone gets excited about a different aspect of staying away overnight. So what can you do to make it a really pleasurable stay?

PREPARE THE BEDROOM

You may never iron the sheets, quilt cover and pillowcases that go in your own bedroom but do make the effort to iron them for your guests. Be sympathetic in your choice of colour and style – if a woman will be using the room, feel free to use linen with lace. Alternatively, if the occupant is going to be male, stick with simple unadorned cotton kit, and no frills. Make sure that you give your guests plenty of

Here's an idea for you... **If the idea of putting a chocolate on the pillowcase is not appropriate for your guests, you can still provide some treats. A selection of wrapped sweets in a small bowl on the bedside table is a lovely touch, as is leaving a small tin of shortbread or assorted biscuits on a table somewhere in the room. Failing that, leave a small fruit basket. Many mail order companies that sell housewares now include tiny fridges in their range of goods. Why not invest in one so that you can leave water, fruit juice or, as a surprise, your guests' favourite tipple in miniature?**

pillows. Synthetic ones are so inexpensive these days that maybe you could invest in a couple of new ones for the occasion. If you plan on putting a couple of spares in the wardrobe remember to use pillowcases that will match the set dressing the bed.

Once the linen is on the bed, dress it up. Layer a throw across the bed or fold an eiderdown so that it sits across the bottom in winter. Pile a few cushions on top of the pillows (raid the living room if you don't have any spares upstairs), and in the winter months finish with a hot water bottle on the bed. It may be that your guests will not want to use it, but it's a considerate touch to give them that option.

There are a few more items that will bring the bedroom up to hotel standard:

- If there is a wardrobe in the room, make sure that you clear it of any other clothes and leave several wooden hangers in place for trousers or skirts, and padded ones for jumpers and shirts.

- Iron any outfits that you will be wearing while your guests are in residence before they arrive. That way you can tuck the iron and ironing board into the wardrobe for them to use as and when they need it.

  > With guests coming to stay you also want to dress up the bathroom: see IDEA 26, *Bathing beauties*, on how to add a touch of luxury to this space.

  Try another idea...

- Make sure that there is a reading light in the room – if it hasn't been used for a while, check that the bulb is working.
- Put a collection of scented candles in the room.

Some people like to sleep in a cool room with the window open, and others like to cocoon themselves in a warm environment. It is worth finding out which option your guests prefer so that you can turn the radiator on or off as required, supply an electric blanket if needed and make sure that the key to the window locks is to hand.

Presumably you have invited these people to stay because you wish to enjoy their company, but that doesn't have to mean being together all day. Consider putting plenty of books (on assorted themes), magazines and a radio or a TV in the guestroom; sometimes they may need their own space.

> '*Lying in bed would be an altogether perfect and supreme experience if only one had a coloured pencil long enough to draw on the ceiling.*'
> G.K. CHESTERTON

Defining idea...

How did it go?

Q **Well, it all sounds ideal if I had the space, but my home office has to double as the guest bedroom, which is hardly luxurious. Any suggestions on how I can dress it up?**

A *One of the best ways to disguise an office is with the clever use of a screen and subtle lighting. For the duration of your guests' stay, place a folding screen in front of your desk and filing cabinet. Exchange a pendant light for one or two lamps fitted with low wattage bulbs, and change your anglepoise lamp for something more appropriate. You probably won't have room for a wardrobe or dress rail so put a hat stand in the room, with a selection of pretty hangers, and a lavender bag or rose-scented pocket hanging from one of the arms.*

Q **OK, but my shelves are stuffed full with all sorts of papers, assorted files and books and they look a real mess. What can I do about this?**

A *My first piece of advice would be to set aside time before your guests arrive to have a clear out; it probably needs one anyway. Alternatively, if that is not on the cards, then you can achieve small miracles with the ready-made muslin panels that are now widely available. Use double-sided tape to hold them in place over your shelves if it's going to be a temporary measure, or pin them up with a staple gun if you plan to keep them there to disguise your mess on a more permanent basis.*

15

The time to dine

Here's a foolproof guide to planning a dinner party at home.

There is one truism about most forms of catering in your own kitchen...

Whether it's a large birthday bash or a small select dinner party for six, there is an easy way to do things and there is a hard way to do things. The easy way is to be organised and plan the whole thing. The hard way is to throw everything together at the last minute. Please try and follow the first!

Think about the type of dinner party that you wish to give.

Here's the first option. You plan to produce a full, five-course affair complete with perfect table settings, the correct wine glasses and a selection of china for every dish. You will be looking to prepare a really special meal, so you'll need plenty of preparation time and will be in and out of the kitchen making sure that the food is just perfect. This will involve you planning and practising the dishes and possibly even printing up a menu that will be presented on the table. The plan is to have a formal meal, so guests should understand that they are expected to dress up. However, you are looking at it as an opportunity to socialise, so while the food will be carefully prepared, you won't be spending most of the meal flitting in and out of the kitchen getting the various courses ready. You'll present some tried and tested dishes that are the staples of your culinary art.

Here's an idea for you...

There is a huge difference between cooking fillets of sole for two and having to prepare the dish for eight or ten people. Here's another example: unless you have the skills of a Michelin-starred chef, and all the equipment and staff of a professional kitchen, the chances are that you will not be able to prepare fillet steaks to suit the desires of eight different people: blue, medium rare, medium well done, etc. It is much easier serving some kind of casserole.

Then there's the second option: a relaxed and casual affair designed so that everyone can sit around, quaff some lovely wine and chow down on a simple dinner that may only consist of two courses. The table settings will be casual and the mood relaxed. For example, people may hang onto their cutlery after eating the starter and use the same ones when the next course appears on the table. The ideal food here would be something like an avocado, mozzarella and tomato starter with some garlic bread and then a lovely spaghetti bolognaise, presented in huge bowls, from which guests will help themselves.

Your decision about which type of event to host will be influenced by how much time you want to spend in the kitchen during the evening. If you hate the idea of everyone else gossiping while you are slaving over a hot stove, then you should be looking at the more casual approach, the second option. If you have only recently started to take cooking seriously but would like the opportunity to practise certain stylish dishes then you might be looking at a blend of the two. And if you really want to show off, are completely confident and know you can set the scene, it's got to be the first option.

Next there are just a few other points to consider:
■ How many courses? (Fewer for casual and more for formal.)
■ What type of food? Do you have to build in provisions for a vegetarian, for example? If you want to spend most of your time at the table, then you have to decide on dishes which can be mostly prepared well in advance.

- Do you have all the right cutlery for the dishes that you want to create? Proper soup spoons, for instance, make all the difference if you are planning soup as a starter.

When serving a variety of drinks, impress your guests with a range of glassware, see IDEA 30, *The class of glass*.

Try another idea...

- How much time will you have beforehand to prepare the food? Unless you are going to take time off from work, choose a Saturday or Sunday night when you have a full day to prepare.
- Do you have both red and white wine glasses? Do you have water tumblers?
- Can any of the courses be served in oven-to-tableware so that people can help themselves from a central pot?

Once you have planned your menu, write a comprehensive list of all the ingredients, even if it is just a sprinkling of salt. Then go through your cupboards and group together any ingredients that you already have in store. Don't take the easy way out and head for the supermarket: find a butcher for the meat, a fishmonger for the shellfish and a deli for the cheese. One tip: before you head to the shops check out food suppliers on the web. If you have never bought food this way, it is a real eye-opener to discover just how many ingredients can be delivered fresh to your door.

Now assemble your ingredients; get your knives, pots and pans at the ready and go to work!

'A man seldom thinks with more earnestness of anything than he does of his dinner.'
SAMUEL JOHNSON

Defining idea...

How did
it go?

Q   You mention preparing everything in advance but can you give me some idea on what this might involve?

A   *Yes, of course. Puddings are one of the easiest courses to prepare beforehand especially if the dish is frozen or needs to be left to cool after it is cooked; salads can be assembled, but not dressed. Obviously, where meat or fish needs marinating you should do that the night before, and many casseroles are actually much better the day after being cooked – the flavours have time to marry together. You'll find guidance in good recipe books.*

Q   Right, I am ready to go, any last minute tips?

A   *Absolutely. Wash up as you go. This reduces the stress. It's a pain, for example, if a knife you need to create your pudding has already been used and you have to excavate it from underneath the heap of unwashed pots in the sink.*

16

Ouch, ouch, ouch

When your eyes open the morning after the party and the light is just too bright, you may need some help.

Here it is...

Of course, many people would argue that if you take the right steps before you start drinking, you will not have to deal with the mother of all hangovers at all. And, of course, there's always the option of not drinking at all – you could be bright-eyed and bushy-tailed and mocking all of your less fortunate friends, who chose to mix grape and grain and are suffering greatly as a result.

There are two or three things that I always try to do before I go out to party. The first is to make sure that I have had a good meal at least two or three hours before going out of the house if there isn't likely to be any food on offer. The second is to have half a glass of water after two or three drinks. And the third is to stick to one type of alcohol.

I know that you have been told this time and time again but pay attention – if you start your evening by drinking beer, then switch to red wine and finish off the night with a brandy or a short, you are cooking up a recipe for disaster.

Here's an idea for you... **Slow down. Try to consume your booze at the rate of one drink an hour. This gives your liver time to break down the alcohol and means you are less likely to suffer the morning after.**

Now, this may not sound very appetising, but I have developed a failsafe drink that seems to keep me in a reasonably good condition right through to the end of the evening. It consists of a half pint of San Miguel or American Budweiser served in a pint glass with lots of ice and a couple of pieces of lime. What you are getting is a long drink, which many people prefer and which clearly takes longer to consume than a shot of something. Also the ice dilutes the strength of the alcohol throughout the evening. Try it – you might like it. The other plus is that it is very refreshing.

There is a theory that you should eat a banana before you go to bed after a heavy drinking session. By all means, if you are sober enough to peel the thing then give this a go. Mind you, this does presuppose that you have recently been to the supermarket and have conscientiously stocked up on fruit... Failing that have a pint of water and take a vitamin C tablet, which can help to ease the pain of the morning after. If you don't have any of those, then just drink gallons and gallons of water.

Defining idea... **'My rule of life prescribed as an absolutely sacred rite smoking cigars and also the drinking of alcohol before, after and, if need be, during all meals and in the intervals between them.'**
WINSTON CHURCHILL

Here are some more dos and don'ts:

- Do try a Bloody Mary: 1.5 oz vodka, a tiny splash of sherry, 3 oz tomato juice, 0.5 oz lemon juice, 6 drops Worcestershire sauce, 4 drops tabasco sauce, freshly ground pepper, a dash of celery salt.

If you are a smoker see IDEA 13, Smoke signals, for the etiquette of having a cigarette while you are out drinking.

Try another idea...

- Maybe try a Prairie Oyster: 1 teaspoon Worcestershire sauce, 1 tablespoon tomato juice, a whole egg yolk, 2 dashes vinegar, a dash of pepper. Make sure, when you pour it into the glass, not to break the egg.
- Avoid brewing up a pot of strong coffee. The initial caffeine hit may help in the short term, but you are setting yourself up for a headache of monumental proportions.
- Don't drink cheap liquor or wine. If you carried a chemistry set you could check how many chemicals are in cheap as opposed to expensive booze, but unless you want to do that then stick to a few glasses of a more expensive wine rather than glugging down something that came in a plastic jug.
- Forget about a hair of the dog (Bloody Mary excepted) – having a glass of the same tipple that laid you low – as this may make you feel better for a while, but you'll feel far worse once the initial effects wear off.

So go out and have fun, but wake up the next day bright and breezy – not slow and sickly!

'Taboos, after all, are only hangovers, the product of diseased minds, you might say; of fearsome people who hadn't the courage to live and who under the guise of morality and religion have imposed these things upon us.'
HENRY MILLER

Defining idea...

How did it go?

Q **Tap water just isn't doing the trick and I can't face going to the shops. What can you suggest to help?**

A *Go to your freezer and rummage. If you don't have a pack of frozen peas (you're not going to cook them, you are going to lie down and rest them across your forehead), then get out your ice tray. Put all the cubes into a plastic bag, wrap this in a tea towel and crush them with a rolling pin. Next, take a hand towel and pour the crushed ice along the middle of the towel in a line. Roll or fold the towel into a compress, go back to bed and lie with this on your forehead until it has melted.*

Q **But isn't that going to make the bed all wet?**

A *Of course it is, so then you'll have to get up and change the sheets (which are probably in need of a wash if you slept in them when you were that drunk). Having a job to do will take your mind off your painful head.*

17

Play that funky music

Or choose something else, any style you want...

There are many occasions when you will want to hire a band to play at your party.

Now whether this simply means subtle, background 'wallpaper' music to give a space the right ambiance, or whether it means a full-blown show, don't leave it to chance. If you get it wrong it can influence the event for the worse; get it right and it makes the time pass that much more enjoyably.

The choice of styles is endless, so you might start by considering whether it is the type of event where people are likely to get up and dance or sing along, in which case you'll be looking for a band that includes some good cover songs in their repertoire. Alternatively, if you expect people just to sit and enjoy a performance you might want to consider jazz or blues.

Also you need to think about how important the music will be. In general terms, at weddings and private parties, you'll be looking for a band to take centre stage; at very formal dinners and corporate affairs the music will act as a background to the event. Fortunately different types of bands, by their choice of music, lend themselves to different situations and there are plenty of companies that have any number of alternative groups on their books whose performances can be tailored to your needs. Hit the web and do some research; you'll soon see how

Here's an idea for you...

Pick the type of music to reflect the tunes that are likely to be popular considering the ages of the people who have been invited. Consider classic, Sinatra-style music for wedding anniversaries; look for a band that does covers from the 60s if it's a school reunion from that period. If it's a much younger group, then maybe disco covers are the answer.

much of an influence your choice of band will have on the occasion.

Take one type of music for example: jazz. According to justjazznyc.com: 'Sometimes jazz music can enliven an event with needed pizzazz. For example, a private party might require the music to be more festive, rather than solely background. Here the addition of drums is particularly effective in creating an energy that can get feet tapping. Another event, though, might need the music to be more flexible, first acting as background and then taking on a more central role as the evening progresses. In this instance, the versatile sound of an added saxophone allows the music to better make the transition from the background to the main element of the party.' Quite.

Alternatively at hoptiludrop.co.uk, Atlantic Soul offers the following food for thought: 'Whether it's two... four... six... or eight on the stage, you can look forward to a high-energy show that has to be seen to be believed. There are dazzling dance routines, with costumes to match. Got a 70s event coming up? The six-piece band brings you Hotpants, complete with costumes... wigs... and nifty dance moves from *Saturday Night Fever* ... with the emphasis of 'getting on down'. Your boogie shoes will be worn out from strutting your funky stuff to classics from Le Freak and T Rex together with Classic Cheese from The Bay City Rollers. These guys are on stage to have fun!'

See what I mean?

Here's a checklist of what to consider when choosing your band.

- The number of guests.
- The size of the venue.
- The location of the band – are they going to be playing outside, for example?
- The age of the guests.

See IDEA 23, *Do a little dance,* if you are going to be booking a disco.

Try another idea...

And finally – your budget. The amount you are charged will usually depend on how many hours the band are playing and how many members are required. Other considerations are whether the band will need to hire extra equipment to fulfil your requirements, on which day of the week the event is happening and how far the band has to travel. Are you allowing for any overtime?

And here are some of the questions that the band will need answered.

- What time does the event start and finish?
- How many slots do you want them to play?
- Is there a break for dinner or speeches?
- How do you want them to dress?

Now start going through your CD collection and get to work on deciding what exactly it is that you want to hear playing on your special occasion.

'I was born with music inside me. Music was one of my parts. Like my ribs, my kidneys, my liver, my heart. Like my blood. It was a force already within me when I arrived on the scene. It was a necessity for me – like food or water.'
RAY CHARLES

Defining idea...

Q **OK, I've picked a band but what other things do I need to consider?**

A   *If you have a specific group in mind, then you really need to book them well in advance. You also need to check with the venue that the type of music you have chosen is acceptable and that the venue will be prepared for the band's arrival on the day.*

Q **What will that involve, don't they just turn up and play?**

A   *Erm, there's more to it than that. The venue will need to know the band's arrival time. Are there specific entrances or exits that they will want the band to use? You'll have to let the band know. Are there trolleys to help with loading and unloading the kit and is there going to be an opportunity for them to do a sound check? You want the band to be happy, so clear all of this well beforehand.*

18

Green issues

What to consider when you are catering for vegetarians and vegans.

Don't be a cliché; just say no to nut roast.

My options when catering for vegetarians and vegans are limited. And that's not because I hold strong views about people's choices (which may be health-related ones), it's just because I rarely have the opportunity to cook specifically vegetarian food. I suspect that a lot of people are in this situation. Be honest and confess your ignorance on this matter.

The old view of lentil-stew-eating, hemp-wearing individuals with pale complexions has long been out of fashion. There have been so many meat-related health issues that vegetarianism or veganism seems increasingly like a sensible choice for anyone. If you are going to be cooking for an individual with particular dietary preferences then take the time to understand what they are about.

This will help:
Vegans don't eat meat, poultry and fish, eggs and dairy products. It's possible that a vegan will also avoid honey. To replace milk, vegans often drink soya milk (as do some people who are lactose intolerant) and use tofu which is also derived from soya beans.
Lacto vegetarians exclude meat, poultry, fish and eggs but will eat dairy products.

Here's an idea for you... **While your guest may have told you that they are happy to eat eggs, why not make the effort to buy a pack of organic eggs from free-range chickens? They often taste better, too.**

Lacto-ovo vegetarians don't eat meat, poultry and fish, but do use eggs and dairy products. Lots of vegetarians fall into this category. There is another group to consider: **Fruitarians** exclude all foods of animal origin as well as pulses and cereals. Their diet mainly includes raw and dried fruits, nuts, honey and olive oil.

So, what is the etiquette involved?

Firstly, you do not have to avoid cooking with meat (or fish or poultry) for everyone who is coming. But you shouldn't just serve up the vegetables and leave your vegetarian guest with that; prepare a specific dish. After all, they are just as important as your other guests and shouldn't be made to feel second best: however, do try to avoid the obvious dishes – which they may well cook for themselves – such as roast stuffed peppers and goat's cheese salad. If they haven't contacted you in advance to let you know, then allow them to take the lead in how to cope with the situation. Most people will be gracious about the mistake and take pot luck with what is available.

If you are having guests from all sides of the food spectrum, one of the easiest meals to make that combines vegetarian and meat options is a curry. Take a look at any Indian restaurant's take-away menu and you will see what I mean – the list of vegetarian curries is often just as long, and equally as enticing (even if you do eat meat), as the poultry, fish or meat ones. Just remember that if you are going to cook a lot of different dishes and allow guests to serve themselves, you should cook the vegetarian options in a separate pan to the others. You should also put enough serving spoons on the table so that each dish can have its own; then they won't be used to serve both meat and vegetarian dishes.

Now, as I said earlier, I think it is important to understand what your vegetarian guest's food choice is all about. Not only does it mean spending more time in the vegetable section and avoiding the meat aisle at the supermarket, it also means walking past a good selection of other products that meat eaters consume without thinking twice. Here's what I mean. If you are planning a mousse for dessert, does it list gelatine in the ingredients? This is derived from animals so is unacceptable to both vegans and vegetarians; there are alternatives, such as agar-agar. Eggs may be off limits as well – and that applies to ice cream too. If a recipe calls for a curry paste or Thai sauce, and you're going to buy it, then make sure that your shop-bought bottle doesn't include anchovies or shrimp.

When you have someone who is very strict in their approach, you need to find drinks that are veggie-friendly (so nothing that includes cochineal for colouring; it's made from beetles). You should also consider going to a specialist cheese shop as most cheese is made with rennet – from cows. A specialist supplier will be able to point you in the right direction.

If someone has made a big effort because you are a vegetarian or vegan, it is appropriate to say thanks. See IDEA 12, *I'm much obliged*, for more about sending a thank-you letter.

Try another idea...

'Vegetables are a must on a diet. I suggest carrot cake, zucchini bread, and pumpkin pie.'
JIM DAVIS, creator of Garfield

Defining idea...

79

How did
it go?

Q   **Some of my best friends are vegetarians, but a few of them seem stricter about what they eat than others, so how do I know what's allowed and what's not?**

A   *Look, some people who say they don't drink will have the occasional glass. And let's be honest, a lot of people who claim they don't smoke will sneak a cheeky drag given a couple of glasses of wine and the opportunity. But whatever your friends have said or done in the past, you should assume that they are strict about their diet when you cook for them.*

Q   **No cheating, then?**

A   *Absolutely not. Never fib about the ingredients in a dish. For example, if you used meat stock to make a risotto, even if it's a mushroom risotto, then you must be honest. If they're not very strict then they may decide to eat it, but the choice must be theirs.*

19

It's a messy business...

But someone's got to do it. Clear up.

Detritus, that's the word. Mess, leftovers, dirt, butts and beer cans, it covers the lot.

Please don't just flick through this bit! In as much as planning an event is vital to its success, so having a clear idea of what you are going to have to do after the balloons have all been popped is nearly as important to your enjoyment of the party.

Put it this way – have an exit plan. The first rule of which is this: don't expect anyone who has consumed more than their fair share of the booze to offer any practical help at all when it comes to cleaning up. Sadly, you may have to put up with them offering moral support along the lines of 'You can take that can, it's full of cigarette butts', or 'I'll just collect the glasses', which means they are off to trawl for any leftover drinks.

Let's deal with the practicalities of restoring order to your home once the party is over.

Don't put off doing the tidying up. You may not feel like cleaning the morning after, but the longer you leave it, the worse it will be. Much worse. You know it.

Here's an idea for you...

After a party, when people have been smoking and drinking in the house, you may have lingering unpleasant odours. You can buy scented products that you put inside your vacuum cleaner which gently perfume the room as you clean up.

So what's the occasion?
Dinner party?
Cocktails?
Full-blown, 'no prisoners' orgy? Well, let's not address the 'orgy' bit, but take it to mean a really good 'dancing till the early hours, drinking the cabinet dry, unexpectedly having to put friends up in the spare room' evening at home.

DINNER PARTIES

As any good chef will tell you, it's important to clean up as you go along. Help yourself by preparing certain elements of the meal the day before so that you can wash up the mixer, blender, bowls and knives you used to create your masterpiece. On the night itself ensure that by the time your guests arrive, the dishwasher is empty, the sink is clear and there is a dedicated space on the work surface where anything cleared away between courses can be deposited.

As you serve up each course, deal with the pots and pans that were used to prepare it. That may mean putting them in the dishwasher (out of sight, out of mind) but if it involves leaving them to soak, make sure the sink is full of lots of hot soapy water.

Don't try and do everything. If guests offer to bring out plates, then let them help. As much as anything, this gives people the chance to take a break from the table and have a breather between courses. This is why it is important to have a space cleared on the work surface where anything dirty can be stacked. You don't want them piled up in the space you need to prepare the next course.

COCKTAILS

Always provide nibbles or canapés when you are serving cocktails to guests. Whether it is cheese straws, or nuts and crisps, it is essential that people can pick at treats to counteract the effect of the alcohol. So there will be some plates, but the main job here will be the reams of glasses that you get through. If you have a dishwasher then the best way to ensure the glasses come out shiny and bright is to wash them on their own. Save everything else and do them on a separate cycle. If you hand-wash glasses then make sure the water is clean and very hot, and use rubber gloves when you are washing up; it really is worth keeping a pair for this job, even if you don't normally use them, so that you can have the water as hot as you can get it. The ideal situation is to have a double sink (or two-bowl arrangement) so that you can wash the glasses in the first and rinse them in the second.

You may need to rearrange the house when hosting an event; check out IDEA 39, *Room to party*, on preparing your home.

Try another idea...

FULL-BLOWN PARTY

Part of clearing up after these types of events may well be to open all the windows wide to clear the atmosphere. Then I suggest you tackle the job room by room, starting with the kitchen. Line up two bin bags, one for food leftovers and cigarette butts and the other for rubbish, and two boxes, one for cans and one for bottles. Have a damp cloth and a dry tea towel at the ready and when you clear a surface, wash and dry it as you go. Leave vacuuming and rearranging the furniture until everything else has been tidied up.

Now get to work!

'Only put off until tomorrow what you are willing to die having left undone.'
PABLO PICASSO

Defining idea...

How did it go?

Q **Wouldn't it be more sensible to concentrate on clearing all the bottles and cans out of every room first?**

A *The reason that I suggest doing a room at a time is that it can be very disheartening to keep walking backwards and forwards through lots of mess, particularly if you are a little the worse for wear. However, if you can at least go into a clean kitchen then you can make tea and toast, or cook bacon and eggs, without having to look at brimming ashtrays and dirty glasses.*

Q **So what comes after the kitchen?**

A *Next tackle all the corridors and passageways. People leave cans on stairs and glasses on windowsills and you don't want to knock these over as you travel to and from the lounge or dining room. Then do the rest.*

20

Dressed to kill

Whether it's fancy dress or a formal affair, what should you wear?

There is nothing worse than arriving at an event and realising that you have chosen completely the wrong outfit.

I think it is easier for women to get it wrong than men, because a man can bluff his way through most situations in a suit and tie: if you feel overdressed you simply remove the jacket and tie and you instantly look less formal. However, if a woman turns up in a little black dress accessorised with gorgeous jewels and everyone else has shown up in jeans, then it takes a great deal of composure to carry off the outfit without embarrassment. Of course, the first thing to do would be remove some of the glitter, but you are still going to stand out.

If you have received an invitation in the post, then the chances are that the dress code will be indicated on the card. Black tie means formal dress. Here's a note for men – don't try out a tie or waistcoat that features cartoon characters or comedy motifs. It may have seemed funny when you looked at it in the shop, but you'll probably regret wearing it when everyone else in the room has adhered to the traditional black tuxedo, white dress shirt and black bow tie. Not only that but you may well embarrass your date. Unless you are tall and slim, don't do a Bogart in

Here's an idea for you...

For women: when choosing a dress for a ball, wedding or party, pick a style that suits your build. If you are short or have a full figure, you might consider something 'empire line', which, with the seam just under the bust, means that the flowing fabric below is complementary to your shape. If you are tall and slim then a long, form-fitting dress can look stunning. Chubby arms look best in long loose sleeves; if you are quite bony, opt for fitted three-quarter length sleeves.

Casablanca and wear a white jacket; black is always more flattering on most men. And here's a note for women. Check with one or two friends or female members of your family to find out what they are going to wear so that you can gauge the style of your outfit accordingly. I'm not saying that you shouldn't be able to wear what you like, within reason, but you will be more comfortable if you fit in with others.

It is particularly important at weddings that men stick to the style that has been indicated and that women do not wear anything that will detract or take the focus away from the bride. You may think this seems a little boring, but you must bear in mind that you are probably going to be photographed with the couple. You do not want the bride and groom to be disappointed with their wedding album just because your outfit stands out in every picture.

Defining idea...

'Clothes make the man. Naked people have little or no influence on society.'
MARK TWAIN

The most important thing about following any dress code is that you feel happy and confident in what you are wearing. Don't vamp it up in your style of dress, if that's not the kind of person that you are. And don't think that you can rely on a couple of glasses to give you Dutch courage. Being tipsy and unhappy with how you look is twice as bad as being sober and unsure.

FANCY DRESS

If you have very little notice, see IDEA 38, *At the last minute*, for some tips on what to wear.

Try another idea...

These parties can be a tremendous success, with the photos passed around for months after the event, or they can be a damp squib if people don't join in. So if you are going to ask people to dress up, make sure that everyone who is invited knows about it – and make sure they know that coming in 'normal' party clothes is unacceptable. There is nothing worse than donning a bunny outfit and walking into a room – or garden in the case of Bridget Jones – when most of the other people haven't 'turned out'. As a guest, the best way to avoid this happening is to go and hire outfits with a group of friends so that you know there'll be safety in numbers.

If you are going to throw a fancy dress party it makes it a simpler prospect for people to decide what to wear if you give the evening a theme. Heroes and Villains is always a good one and Nursery Rhymes provides plenty of scope if there are going to be children at the party too.

Whatever the choice, party gear or fancy dress, plan your outfit well in advance to avoid last minute panics and the possibility that 'you don't have anything to wear'!

'Clothes and manners do not make the man; but when he is made, they greatly improve his appearance.'
ARTHUR ASHE

Defining idea...

87

How did
it go?

Q **I know that I have to be smart but I am confused about the difference between black tie and white tie. Can you straighten this out?**

A *Black tie means that you are expected to wear a tuxedo whereas white tie indicates that the man should wear a tail coat (which is one step up from a dinner jacket in the formal stakes) and a white tie. 'White tie' is more formal.*

Q **Right, that's me sorted – but what about my date?**

A *White tie for ladies indicates that they should consider wearing something long and glamorous; it's not appropriate to wear a short dress to something where white tie is specified. Black tie simply means a smart look – it could be a two-piece outfit like an evening trouser suit or a smart, cocktail-type dress.*

21

An illuminating idea

Guests will relax when the lighting is just right.

There is no bigger blow at the end of a party than when someone decides to turn all the lights on full beam.

Talk about a shock – especially if you are in a dark corner taking liberties with someone. I can understand that it is the easiest way to get everyone to clear a room, but it's not pleasant. My suggestion would be to turn off the music and then send someone from group to group to guide people towards the exit. It might take longer but it would be a much more relaxing way to finish the night.

But what are the options for lighting your party in the first place?

Go to any party organiser and they will have a plethora of lighting options. The most important point is to be clear on the mood that you want to create. Perhaps there are different elements to your event – say cocktails and then a sit-down dinner with speeches, and then dancing. All of these elements would benefit from different lighting: bright when people arrive, slightly more subtle light over dinner, something brighter when people need to be able to see the speakers – and then a moody light to finish off the night.

Here's an idea for you... **If you regularly use your garden for barbecues and parties, consider employing a garden lighting expert to put together a scheme for you. Think about the area as an extra room: you might have lamps, pendant lights and uplighters to illuminate different areas of your lounge, and you can do this in the garden too. You might consider bulbs set into the walls or patio floor, and put individual lights in your flowerbeds to draw the focus to particularly impressive plants. A professional will come up with a complete scheme that will transform the look of the space.**

Another thing to consider with your choice of lights is whether there are any focal points at the event. For example, you may have an ice sculpture that you want highlighted or a display of awards that are going to be handed out later. If there is a stage for a band or disco, you may need to be able to control the lighting in their set-up area independently of the rest of the room.

Modern technology allows experienced party organisers to show you how their different lights will look in a virtual mock-up of your event. So what are the different areas that you need to consider?

Here are some examples:

- Do you want spotlights that can be turned on particular tables?
- Would you like coloured gels that will 'warm' or 'cool down' a room?
- Is it an idea to have a set of flashing lights over the dance floor?
- Do you want chandeliers to make a dramatic impact as part of the overall decor?
- Is there a blank wall where you could project the company logo?

And, if you are going to be outside as well as inside, can you have garden torches, sweeping beams, lanterns in trees or fairy lights included in the overall list of lights?

If you are entertaining at home, it is still important to consider different effects, depending on which spaces are being used. It is always a good idea to make sure that there is a light at the front of the house that illuminates your house number or name. This is particularly important if you are throwing a housewarming party or have invited people who have never been to your home before. Once inside, keep a strong light in the hallway. Moving through the rooms, make sure that you have wall lights that can be used in the lounge or a dimmer switch on your ceiling pendant light so that the room is not overly bright. If you have a downstairs cloakroom, it makes a lovely touch to have this lit by a group of tea lights. (Make sure that they are in safe containers and remember to check on them regularly.) If you are serving food in a buffet, you want people to be able to see what they are choosing to eat: instead of putting the food in the lounge, use the kitchen table where you can keep the light a little brighter without ruining the atmosphere elsewhere. If this is where you are keeping the drink, then it has the added advantage that people can see what they are drinking too.

Don't forget the back garden or patio even in winter. If you have the budget – and they are coming down in price – I would strongly recommend investing in a patio heater, the light from which gives a wonderful glow. You can also use large pots filled with sand to support garden flares. Trees decked out in fairy lights look wonderful but make sure that you buy lights that are specifically recommended for use outside.

If you've left your lighting until the last minute, you've probably put off doing other things too. See IDEA 38, *At the last minute*, for some help.

Try another idea...

'Freedom is just Chaos, with better lighting.'
ALAN DEAN FOSTER, author

Defining idea...

How did it go?

Q **I don't have a dimmer switch on the lounge light but I do want to have the lighting in there turned down low. Is there any way of achieving this?**

A *You have two options. The first is to replace all the bulbs in your ceiling fitting with ones of a lower wattage than you'd normally use. Secondly, if the bulbs are not visible to the naked eye, you could simply remove one or two depending on how many there are in the fitting.*

Q **I don't have time to get to the shops. The lights still aren't right – what can I do?**

A *Go round your home and steal the lamps from the bedroom or study. Take these downstairs and arrange them in the lounge. If they are floor-standing lights then try and tuck them in the corners of the room where they will not get in everyone's way; if they are table lamps then put them on bookshelves or on side tables positioned at the edges of the room.*

22

Making a mark

Accidents can happen, and if wine or food gets spilled then the best solution is to clear things up quickly.

I can't emphasise the timing enough!

Getting a surface clean isn't just about what has been spilled, it is about what it has been spilled on and how long it has been there. A dropped glass of red wine is a potential nightmare if spilled on a pale carpet or a pristine white tablecloth. Coffee can leave a mark, even if it is quickly cleared up. It's a bore when something gets spilled at a party but having quick reactions will make the chore of cleaning up that much easier.

How do you tackle the job? There are dozens of different proprietary products available in the shops, and many different approaches that you can take. Whatever you use, it always helps if you know what caused the stain in the first place, as a treatment that might clear up one spill could set another stain in its place.

So, rule one is to act quickly and rule two is to remove as much of the spilled item as possible before you treat it with anything. When it is a liquid spill, then blot it with kitchen towel or an absorbent cloth. Don't rub at the stain, whatever you do. If it's on a carpet, for example, you will only be working it further into the surface. If whatever has been spilled is solid, spoon up as much as you can and then use the blunt side of a knife to scrape up the rest. Don't use the sharp side as this may cause damage. Before treating any stain, test the solution you are using on a hidden or inconspicuous part of the surface.

Here's an idea for you...

If you have a sheet, quilt cover or pillowcase that is old and faded and you were going to throw it out, think again. Take the time to cut the fabric into pieces (about 50 cm x 50 cm) and put them in a bag with your cleaning materials. That way whenever you do need to clean up a stain, you will have plenty of cloths to hand that can be thrown away afterwards.

Now let's get more specific and look at some common culprits...

There's beer on the carpet.
Step 1: Mix a teaspoon of a neutral detergent (a mild detergent containing no alkalis or bleaches) with a small jug of warm water and blot the stain.
Step 2: Mix a third of a cup of white household vinegar with two-thirds of a cup of water and blot the stain.
Step 3: Sponge the area with a clean cloth and clean water and blot the area again. Leave it to dry before you vacuum.

Someone cut themselves and there's blood on the sofa.
Step 1: Mix a teaspoon of a neutral detergent with a cup of lukewarm water and then blot.
Step 2: Mix a tablespoon of household ammonia with half a cup of water and then blot.
Step 3: Sponge with clean water and blot again.

Bread has been dropped, butter side down, on the rug.
Step 1: After lifting any remnants, sponge the area with a small amount of dry-cleaning solvent and blot. (Use small amounts to prevent any possible damage to the backing of the rug.)
Step 2: Mix one teaspoon of a neutral detergent with a cup of warm water and blot.

There's candle wax on the floor.

Step 1: Take a piece of plain paper and lay it over the wax. Take your iron and put it on a warm setting, then iron the paper; you'll see the wax coming through. Keep moving the iron – leave it on one spot and you could melt the carpet fibres.

Step 2: Sponge the area with a small amount of dry-cleaning solvent.

Step 3: Mix one teaspoon of a neutral detergent with a cup of lukewarm water and blot.

A cup of coffee has been kicked over.

Step 1: Mix one teaspoon of a neutral detergent with a cup of lukewarm water and blot the area.

Step 2: Mix a third of a cup of white household vinegar with two-thirds of a cup of water and blot the area again.

Step 3: Sponge the area with clean water.

Red wine has stained the tablecloth.

Step 1: Mix one teaspoon of a neutral detergent with a cup of lukewarm water and blot the stain.

Step 2: Mix a third of a cup of white household vinegar with two-thirds of a cup of water and blot it once more.

Step 3: Repeat step one.

Step 4: Sponge the surface with clean water and then wash the cloth as soon as possible.

Act quickly, and be thorough, and stains should be easily removed.

If you do spill something, always tell your host. See IDEA 44, *The good guest guide*, for more tips on good behaviour.

Try another idea...

'What is laid down, ordered, factual is never enough to embrace the whole truth: life always spills over the rim of every cup.'
BORIS PASTERNAK

Defining idea...

95

How did
it go?

Q I have acted quickly on a red wine stain on the carpet but there is still a mark. What do I do next?

A *The best approach is to keep on repeating the process you used. It may be that the wine has worked its way into the carpet fibres and you'll need two or three goes before it finally lifts.*

Q And if that doesn't work?

A *Use a disguise! Can you move a piece of furniture so that it covers the stain, or is there a rug in the room which could be placed in position to conceal that part of the carpet?*

Q Honestly? The red wine stain is just one of many marks. It was a great party but the floor looks terrible. What now?

A *If it really is that bad then it's time to call in a professional cleaner. Make sure that you know the dimensions of the room and then ring a few companies and get a quote. Be honest about the condition of the flooring and mention any specific marks and stains. Also, bear in mind that when one room is cleaned it may make others look worse. Is it time to have the whole place professionally cleaned?*

23

Do a little dance

Bring on the disco music when you want to strut your stuff all night.

Dancing can be one of the best things at a wedding or other event — but you do have to get it right. Here's how.

Nine times out of ten, wedding discos are fantastic. There's a range of music for all ages, the DJs are happy to take requests and people from three or four generations can bob away to their hearts' content without the fear of feeling foolish. No one cares how silly they might look; they just enjoy themselves.

The first thing I want you to understand is that there is no point in booking a DJ based on the cost alone. You may have already spent lots of money on catering and cars, outfits and invitations, but hire a cheap DJ and you could face the following situations:

- The equipment that they use may not be top quality, so the sound that you hear will be inferior.
- They may not have insurance.
- They may not have a very wide selection of music.
- It could be that they are just not very good and they don't know how to get a dancefloor going.
- They may not worry about how they are dressed.

Here's an idea for you... **Although it might be the unluckiest thing that could happen, there is always a possibility that your DJ could be taken ill or that the equipment could fail. If you want to cover yourself against such a disaster, why not think about booking a DJ through an agency, which has many different people on their books? That way, in order to cover yourself against something going wrong, you can negotiate a backup plan when you sign the contract.**

In no situation is the saying 'if you pay peanuts, you get monkeys' more apt than with a bad DJ. Almost everyone has been at an event where the *Sounds of the Sixties* compilation mix is the most contemporary music that the DJ has – and, boy, do people remember a party when the music's been crap. So what should you take into consideration when looking for a real pro?

You might think that the first question should be about the music and you might be right, but in my experience it is better to start by asking them about their equipment. If their set-up is two old turntables and a single set of flashing lights, it's an indication that they might be a cheap outfit and that the resulting service could be poor. An impressive set-up indicates that they will perform well on the night, and if they can show you videos of previous events then so much the better. Part of good presentation is how the DJ will be dressed, so make it clear if you want something smarter than jeans and a T-shirt. You may also want to make sure that their equipment has been safety tested within the last year. If you are happy that they are going to 'put on a show' then move on to the music.

Defining idea... '**Dancing is a sweat job.**'
FRED ASTAIRE

You will know the type of tunes that you want to dance to, so think about making up a rough playlist before you speak to the DJ. If nothing on your list matches anything in their collection then it is clear that you are on a

See IDEA 46, *The perfect host*, for other things you need to think about when planning your event.

Try another idea...

different wavelength, which is no starting point for a good working relationship. If you are after a particular type of music, then ask the DJ what they have in that genre. Don't dictate every tune for the night; by all means provide them with the equivalent of 50–60% of the music for their set, but the reason you are paying them is for their skills so allow them to judge the rest. For more formal events you may also want to discuss with them what is available for the first and last dance of the night. It's vital that you agree the latter because you really don't want to end up with *Hi, Ho, Silver Lining*…

On a very practical note, make sure that your DJ has insurance. Let's hope that no one dancing trips over a cable and hurts themselves, but accidents do happen and it is essential that you are covered should something occur. Make sure that you see your DJ's certificate before you sign any booking form.

Now you are ready to choose your music man, so get your dancing shoes on and get ready to party.

'Disco dancing is just the steady thump of a giant moron knocking in an endless nail.'
CLIVE JAMES

Defining idea...

How did
it go?

Q   You mentioned signing contracts but a friend of a friend who is going to DJ says not to worry about it. Why do I need one?

A   *How would you like everyone to turn up and find no music? When you have a signed contract stating the date and time and location of the gig then the DJ is legally obliged to turn up. Also your fee will be written down in black and white plus, more importantly, the DJ's overtime rates. If the party venue allows you to carry on a little after the official closing time, you may want your DJ to continue playing; if you have a written confirmation of overtime rates then you won't end up paying an extortionate amount. (Remember you will need to clear any extra time with the manager of your venue.)*

Q   Will I be expected to pay them on the night?

A   *The DJ will probably have asked you for a deposit when you made the booking for the event, which might be as much as 50%, but yes, you will have to settle the balance on the night. Make sure that you get receipts even if you are paying them cash in hand.*

24

Help is at hand

Hiring caterers and bar staff can take the pressure off you.

Of course, if you're hosting a large event then you'll need help. There are companies that will take all the stress out of catering, so use them when you can.

Whether you actually go down this route has a lot to do with your available budget. You will probably be paying per head so work out whether you would like to have fewer people and have your party catered or invite more guests and do all the hard work yourself. What are the advantages of hiring help?

One of the main reasons for using a company to cater your event is that they will supply all the equipment necessary for the party. That could be all the crockery, cutlery and table linen, or it might be all the glasses and assorted drinks that you are going to need. If you decide that you want to buy the booze yourself, you'll probably be charged for the bottles that they open. Another plus is that they will deal with the clearing up. Be clear on when you want this to take place. If, for example, you are going to have speeches at the party, you want as little movement from the waiting staff as possible when these are taking place. So make sure they will either have finished clearing up, or that they will wait until everyone has

Here's an idea for you... **Ask your caterer to put together a selection of different wines for your event and make sure that you go and have a tasting. Be clear about the type of wine that you want: whether it is light, full bodied or oaky. If you are not an expert then ask for their wine buyer to contact you to discuss the options available.**

finished speaking before they begin. Additionally, you may be able to call on them to provide a master of ceremonies so that he/she can introduce a speaker or indicate toasts.

Right, you're going to use help. What steps do you need to follow?

- Ask around among friends and colleagues before hiring a company. Someone may have recently attended a party where the food and drink was fantastic or where the level of service stood out.
- Call any companies on your 'possibles' list and check that they are free on the date of your event.
- Find out if the company has a similar event already booked in and whether you can pop in to see them in action.
- Get a list of references and check them thoroughly.
- Narrow your choice down to two and compare everything.
- Have their chef draw up a sample menu.
- Arrange a meeting to confirm all the details and get a contract drawn up with everything agreed.
- Check in with the company the week before the event and then again the day before it takes place.

Defining idea... **'Treat employees like partners, and they act like partners.'**
FRED ALLEN, comedian

When you decide that you are going to use outside help, book your caterers well in advance and give yourself time for them to get to know you and vice versa. The more that they know about you, the better they will be able to judge the mood of the event. If you are quite a laid-back, unfussy and relaxed person then the staff that do the job can, while still approaching the job professionally, reflect that

For how to budget, see IDEA 34, *The price is right*, which will help you decide if you want to bring in caterers.

Try another idea...

in their approach. If you are a more formal person (or if the occasion is more formal) you can make it absolutely clear that you aren't expecting any levity from anyone concerned.

Here's an example of how getting to know your caterer can really work. Simon, a chef friend, told me that he was employed to cater a wedding and asked the groom if he had any favourite foods. The groom replied that he loved scallops. Now Simon knew that providing scallops for a large group of people wasn't an option: firstly, because it would prove very expensive and secondly, because you don't serve something unusual unless you know most people will eat it. They settled on a more simple dish. However, Simon served the groom with his own special scallop starter at the wedding breakfast and he was thrilled, as you can imagine.

WHAT DO YOU NEED?

Depending on the type of event that you are hosting you may want to consider employing any of the following: bartenders, waiting staff, a coat checker and chefs. As the host of the event, do try and meet all the people who are going to be working at your party. It will help them to do their job in accordance with your wishes.

'The magic formula that successful businesses have discovered is to treat customers like guests and employees like people.'
TOM PETERS, American business guru

Defining idea...

Q **I've received a sample menu from the company I want to use, but it works out more expensive than I expected to pay per head. What do I do?**

A *That's fine, you don't have to agree to it just because it's their recommendation. There are all sorts of ways of reducing the costs, including changing a more expensive ingredient in a dish for a cheaper one or maybe reducing the number of options if you have indicated a choice of starters, main courses and desserts for your meal.*

Q **Won't they think I'm being a bit of a cheapskate?**

A *You really don't need to worry. If they are any good, the company that you are going to employ will want to create a good impression so they will be happy to accommodate your needs. Can I just suggest that the quickest way to bring down costs is to change your choice of wine or beer? Ask if you can opt for a house wine and request draught beer rather than bottles.*

25

The iceman cometh

Ice sculptures can be themed to provide a stunning focal point for any event.

The idea of drinking freezing cold vodka that has just been sent down a shoot of ice may not appeal to everyone, but boy does it taste good.

Vodka should be drunk at that temperature anyway, which is why you need to keep it in the freezer at home. Now I am not saying that the only reason to include an ice sculpture at your event is so that you can have a vodka luge, because there are lots of other shapes, styles and reasons why you might want to have one. But it sure gives a kicking start to your event!

If you haven't seen one, an ice luge is a fantastic device for delivering ice-cold spirit from the bottle via a channel into the lucky – or worse for wear – recipient's mouth. A channel is carved through the ice into which the vodka is poured. You mustn't let over-zealous guests pour drinks with a low alcohol content through the luge; the spirit used must have a high alcohol content to prevent it blocking the shoot.

Here's an idea for you... **If you are planning an event for your company ask the ice-sculpting company to carve your logo in ice. It will make a stunning centrepiece for a head table or buffet and you can ask for it to be lit in the company colour.**

Here's how leading ice-sculptor Jonathan Lloyd once described one of his more imaginative creations to me: 'You put the vodka in one arse and drink it out of the other.' This may sound like a bit of a startling proposition, but it was his 'Fall of the Damned' design that offered this particular possibility. It featured two entwined bodies, legs in the air, descending into the flames of hell. It gives you some idea of just how creative ice sculptors can be. The reason for Jonathan's unusual approach was because he had spent years making one of two classic vodka luge designs: the first a male torso (you drink the vodka out of the penis – one for a hen night, perhaps?) and the second a female one (where you sup your shot from the – well, you can imagine the rest, many bachelor parties request this design) and he wanted to add another twist to the tale.

You can make anything you want in ice. Yes, really – anything. Sounds like an outrageous observation? Then picture this. A life-size, fully working bar, including pool tables, dartboard and barmaid all carved in ice. This was created for brewing giant Guinness. Or how about a racing car made for McLaren? Clearly these projects used vast amounts of ice, a whole team of carvers and had a huge budget – scale things down for your event.

WHAT DO YOU NEED TO KNOW?

The first thing to understand is that an ice sculpture really is made from ice so it will melt during your event. Isn't this a shame? Well, it looks so stunning to begin with that you really won't mind as it gradually disappears. The bigger the form, the longer it will last. It just depends on the temperature in the room and also the size and type of ice sculpture. It usually takes a sculpture a couple of hours to reach the temperature at which it will start to melt. But you can figure on small sculptures starting to lose their detail and disappearing in three to five hours, and medium-sized designs melting gradually over four to six hours. If you choose a really big design, it may last as long as nine or ten hours.

Having a luge adds an element of fun to an event. For more ways to entertain your guests see IDEA 40, *Adult games.*

Try another idea...

HOW IS IT MADE?

Some designs are cast in moulds. Classic pieces like ice vases, swans or a salmon which stands on a buffet table may well have been made in a mould. Ice sculptors work with blocks of ice, chisels and chainsaws to design more individual pieces. You can have a design made to any shape or size, within reason, but the average is about a metre high. They can be pretty heavy but the company that creates them will deliver them and set them up in position.

HOW MUCH NOTICE DO I NEED TO GIVE?

'I am obsessed with ice cubes. Obsessed.'
DREW BARRYMORE

Defining idea...

The rule of thumb is to give the company as much notice as possible, especially for bespoke designs. Many companies take bookings six to twelve months in advance. But bear in mind that when you do book, you will need to pay a 50% deposit in most cases. The balance should be paid on delivery.

If you are looking for a design for a wedding think about some of the following possibilities: entwined hearts, kissing swans, a wedding cake, Cupid, two lovebirds, a heart with flowers and the names of the couple.

If you are having a buffet you could decorate the table with one of these: a fruit bowl, a giant clam, an open scallop, a leaping salmon, a mermaid, a wine rack…

If you are celebrating a particular birthday or anniversary why not order one of these? A champagne bottle, a champagne ice bucket, a candle, an ice pillar with roses, numbers, initials…

How did it go?

Q   It sounds amazing but one thing is worrying me. What happens to the water as it melts?

A   *Don't worry, the floor doesn't get drenched. Drip trays are supplied with ice sculptures and a tube runs into a bucket below the table the sculpture is placed on.*

Q   Doesn't this look a little ugly?

A   *No. The trays themselves are designed to be on display so they won't look out of place on your buffet table, and the bucket is concealed under the table so that it isn't visible to the guests at the event.*

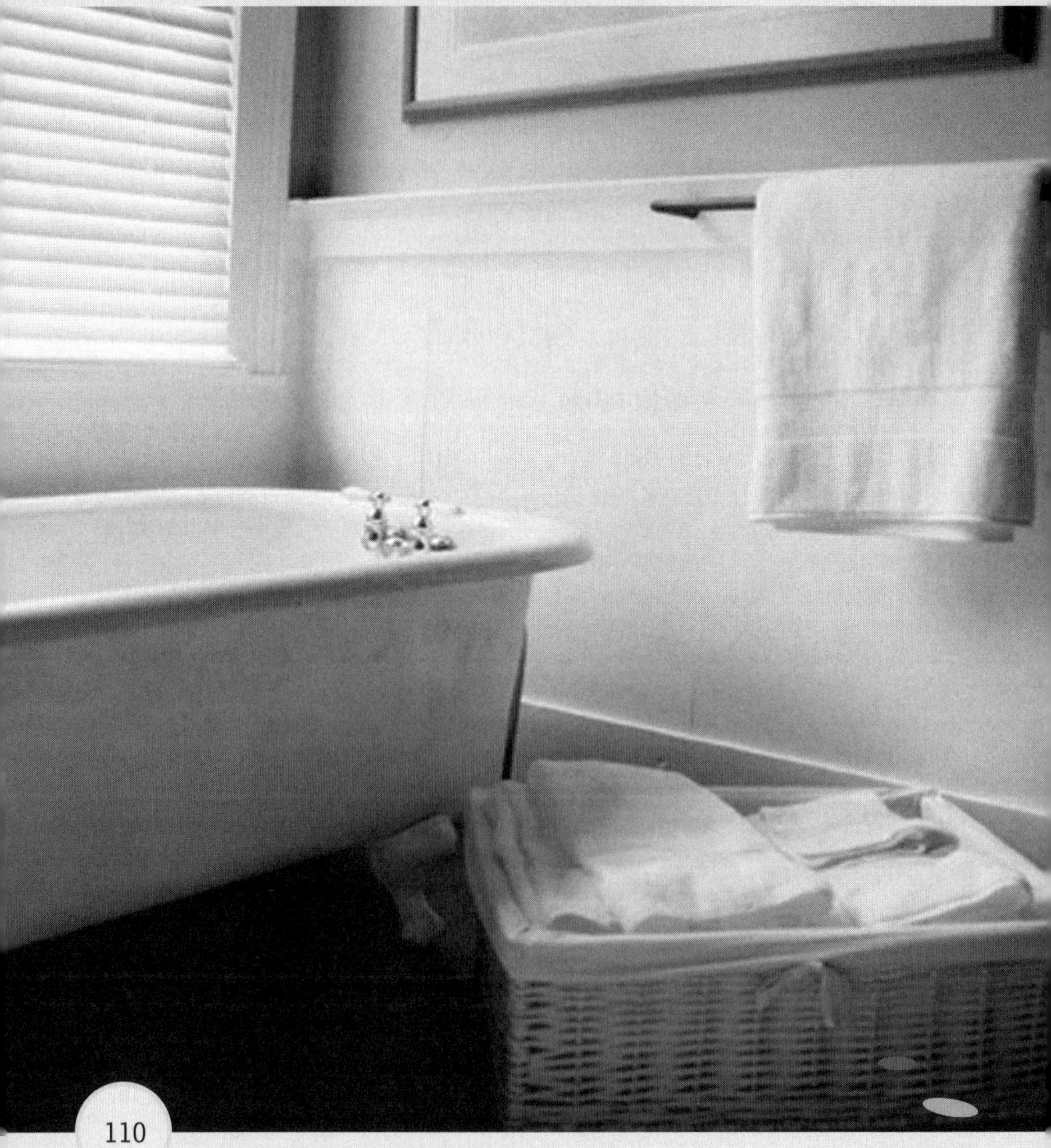

26

Bathing beauties

If guests are coming to stay why not give the bathroom a real facelift?

Think about giving your guests a touch of luxury...

I am always excited when asked to go and stay with my friends Emma and Cliff. Their bathroom is a joy to behold... the shower is a big, walk-in affair. There is no need for a screen or shower curtain because it has been built along such generous lines. And the bath. Oh, the bath. It's deep, really deep and there are no horrible taps to bang your head on. The centrally placed water supply is operated by controls mounted on the wall so you can sit at either end and relax. Underfloor heating means it is always toasty and a heated towel rail means the towels are always warm. It's bliss.

Now, I know what you are thinking: 'I am not going to have my bathroom remodelled just so my guests can bathe or shower in luxury.' Fair point. But what you can do is work with what you have got to deliver a really pleasurable experience.

Where do you start? Clean, clean, clean. First take everything that isn't plumbed in or nailed to the walls out of the room (and that includes the shower curtain if you have one). Use a descaler on any tiles in the room. This is a laborious job, which is why people leave it for months and months before tackling it, which only makes it

Here's an idea for you... **Have you got a packet of cotton slippers, the kind that you are given at health farms or when you travel on long-distance flights? Leave them unopened, tucked into the pocket of the dressing gown. It means that guests can come down to breakfast without having to worry about donning their shoes and socks.**

more like hard work. Once you have cleaned the tiles, tackle the suite. Make sure that the plugholes are cleaned out and that plugs and chains are not harbouring any hair. Descale the showerhead so that it works to its full capacity. Wipe down any shelves. If you have an internal bathroom, make sure that you dust all the light fittings. If you are lucky enough to have a window then ensure that any condensation-caused mildew is cleaned off the glass and windowsill.

Next, clean everything that you have taken out of the room. If you have had your shower curtain for years and it has that horrible slimy mould along the bottom, then chuck it out and invest in a new one. They are so cheap that there is no excuse for living with a bacterial culture growing in your bathroom. (This applies even if you aren't having guests to stay, by the way.)

Take all your half-used toiletries and put them in a box in your own bedroom. Then put fresh bottles of shampoo and conditioner in the room. Choose a product with lovely packaging if you haven't got special holders into which to decant them.

Defining idea... **'Some people think luxury is the opposite of poverty. It is not. It is the opposite of vulgarity.'**
COCO CHANEL

Leave a new tube of toothpaste and a new toothbrush still in its packaging. While your guests will probably bring their own, it is one of those frequently forgotten things that people clearly need. Remember some shaving foam too.

Right, now that has all been sorted, put together the lovely extras, the things which will make it a real treat for your guests to use the room.

Dress up your spare bedroom for guests as well: check out IDEA 14, Be my guest.

Try another idea...

- A clean dressing gown on the back of the door.
- Fluffy towels.
- Candles.
- Essential oils.
- A basket of any face-cream samples, perfumes, face wipes or the assorted goodies that you pick up in hotels and on planes.

Do you have a bathroom cabinet? If you forgot about this in the clean up, then do it now. Clear it out and wipe down all the shelves. Replace the spare soap and toilet rolls, cotton wool buds, nail files, tweezers and put in a fresh packet of disposable razors. Also add some aspirin and an indigestion remedy. It saves a guest having to suffer in silence if these last two items are provided, as some people may be embarrassed about asking for them when they have just consumed your food or too much of your wine.

Think about the people who are staying. If it's someone that you really want to indulge, then also leave a body scrub, new loofah, face packs and body lotions in the room. There is nothing like spoiling a friend to ensure that they will really enjoy their stay.

Indulge your friends when they visit and just think what treats you can look forward to when you make the return trip!

'Luxury is an enticing pleasure, a bastard mirth, which hath honey in her mouth, gall in her heart, and a sting in her tail.'
FRANCIS QUARLES, poet

Defining idea...

How did
it go?

Q **This all sounds lovely but I am going to be using the bathroom too. What about my stuff?**

A *I know that this sounds extreme, but is it too much to ask that you carry your towels and toothbrush into the bathroom in the morning? Clearly you can use all the lovely toiletries that you have put in there, so you really don't need to carry in the box of stuff that you cleared out every time that you want to use the room.*

Q **And this is really necessary?**

A *Put yourself in their position. Wouldn't you be thrilled that someone had gone to all this effort for you? Trust me. One of the loveliest things a friend can do is to provide a treat or something special that is just a little out of the ordinary and that is, also, completely unexpected. The chance for your guests to don a bathrobe so that they do not have to worry about carrying clothes into the bathroom, enjoy a long soak in a pristine bath and then dry themselves on a fluffy towel will mean that they enjoy your hospitality all the more.*

27

Make mine a double

Pull no punches when planning the drinks for your party.

It can be complicated, so here's how to make sure that you have the right amount of alcohol for your event.

We've all been there. It's late at night and the fridge is empty of beer, the cocktail cabinet is a desert and so it is deemed sensible to start on the leftover bottles of red wine. If I had a pound for every person who blames their hangover on a combination of grape and grain, I would be a very rich woman. Estimating the amounts of drink is never going to be easy and your budget is a major factor in the equation.

You can't predict how long people will be around, but I would suggest a good proportion of those invited will last until the end and there's nothing worse than the drinks running out. So be as generous as your wallet permits with your allowance per person. To estimate how much you might need to spend on alcohol, you can expect this to be approximately half as much per person as you spend per person on food.

Here's an idea for you... **If you are concerned about the quantity of alcohol that is going to be consumed, arrange with waiting staff not to leave bottles on the tables. That way you limit automatic refills. It's a fact that people are much more wasteful with wine when it is left on the table rather than when it's being served on request.**

Let's think about drinks at a venue. Some of this applies equally to drinks at home, too. My favourite bar manager, Heddy, has organised the booze and the bar at countless events. His most salient piece of advice is 'know your guests'. He knows that if you have a group combining one or two generations of adults and children at a sit-down dinner, they will generally drink far less than guests at a buffet party of friends celebrating a twenty-fifth birthday.

One of the first decisions that he asks people to make is whether they are going to run an open bar, pay for the wine and beer and allow people to buy their own spirits or whether they want to put a tab behind the bar to cover all drinks. Be clear which option you favour so that there are no misunderstandings on the night.

If you are going to put an amount of money behind the bar then ask the manager to keep you informed about how much money has been spent. I would suggest that you want to know when half of the money has gone and again when about 80% has been spent, so that you can monitor the situation and won't get a shock. Don't tell people how much money is in the kitty, but it can be an idea to mention to one or two close friends that it will revert to a paying bar when the money runs out; this will get round.

Have a discussion with the bar manager about what you want the bar staff to say to guests when the money has actually gone. The best approach is to tell people as soon as they approach the bar rather than wait until they have placed their drinks order.

If you are going to be serving champagne, see IDEA 31, Bubbling over.

Try another idea...

So here are some points to consider:
- Is it a formal occasion? People drink less at a ceremonial affair than during an informal and lively event.
- What time of year is it? In the summer you need to up the amount of soft drinks and beer.
- What time of day is it taking place? You'll need less booze during the day than you will in the evening.
- How old are the people who are coming? Older guests drink less; a younger group will consume more.
- Are you serving food? People also tend to drink less when they are eating.

In general, at a sit-down dinner you should allow two large glasses of wine per person. This is about two-thirds of a bottle of wine and while it doesn't appear to be that much, think of it in these terms: sixty people at the meal equates to a hundred bottles.

'Drinking makes such fools of people, and people are such fools to begin with that it's compounding a felony.'
ROBERT BENCHLEY, author

Defining idea...

If you are buying a lot of wine the advantage is, of course, that you can negotiate on the price per bottle. Remember that you also want to include soft drinks such as juice or cola if there are going to be children at the event. Just a note: if you are going to incorporate toasts, allow two glasses of champagne per person. You can expect to get five glasses per bottle. And please don't be troubled about ordering bottles of mineral water. Ask the staff to put jugs of iced water on the table and instruct them to make sure that they are monitored and refilled as required. This is enough for most people's needs.

Are you planning an evening buffet? Then allow three to four drinks per person for the event. If the party is going to run for a long time, say more than five hours, budget for four to six drinks per guest.

So now you know what you need, get to the bar and order your first drink.

How did it go?

Q   We're having a cocktail party. How many drinks would you suggest?

A   Work on the assumption that your guests will have two drinks per hour for the first couple of hours and then one drink per hour after that.

Q   How many bottles is that?

A   That entirely depends on how many different types of cocktails you are serving but you can expect to get roughly sixteen shots out of the standard bottles of vodka, gin, rum, bourbon, scotch and tequila.

28

Location, location, location...

What are you looking for when you need to hire a venue?

If you are lucky enough to have a huge house, a penthouse apartment or a country estate, you already have the space to throw a party for a substantial number of people. But let's suppose you don't...

For the rest of us mere mortals, who live life in less grandiose environs, there will be plenty of times when we need to find room so that friends or family can party. Depending on the nature of the occasion we may require a smart hotel, a cosy wine bar, a trendy disco, a five-star restaurant or a more unusual place to host our event.

In this last category, be adventurous. It is possible to hire areas at a zoo, an art gallery, a museum or even a tourist attraction. (In London, for example, it is feasible to rent the London Dungeon in the evening where you can enjoy Rocky Horror Parties, Medieval Buffets or Transylvanian Feasts for up to 400 people.) Staying with this criteria, zoos and aquariums are obviously perfect when you want to entertain children, while for a sophisticated set, cocktails in an art gallery is an absolute winner. Here's how the Guggenheim in New York describes one of its spaces: 'The Museum's signature Frank Lloyd Wright building provides several unequalled and

Here's an idea for you...

If you are not wedded to the idea of holding your event on a Friday or Saturday, it is worth looking at the options for a different day of the week. This could provide you with a wider choice of venues, especially if you are arranging something at very short notice. The reason for this is that many places get fully booked for months in advance on the two most popular days of the week. This is especially true at Christmas and during other national holidays.

dramatic spaces for corporate events, including the spacious rotunda floor and the famous quarter-mile spiral ramp winding up to the seventh floor, directly beneath the magnificently restored skylight.' Sounds impressive, doesn't it? It is.

POINTS TO CONSIDER

You want to feel relaxed and happy in the space. When you visit any potential venue, make sure that you get a good vibe from the place. However, the budget has to come first. Make a list of several places that you are considering and do a ring round to get some idea of the costs involved. It will save disappointment, as you get further into the planning process, if you rule out anywhere that may sound and look perfect but is extortionately expensive to hire. Work out the number of guests that you wish to include. As you draw up your list try and add the names in order of priority. Start with those people who must receive an invite, and end with those it would be nice to include but who wouldn't necessarily expect to be there. The number of guests could very easily rule out some venues as, for safety reasons, they will be specific about the maximum number.

Now the details. Decide on the type of drinks that you are going to provide. Does the venue have a bar? What type of food do you wish to serve? Is there scope for a sit-down dinner? Is there an area that would be perfect for laying out a buffet? Will you want trays of canapés to be circulated during the evening? Does the venue have its own caterers or will you need to bring a company in for the event?

Consider whether you want music. If it's a night-time affair, you may want to check whether there is a dance floor or if it's possible to allocate a space for dancing. Or you might need a microphone and space from which a speaker can address the group. Are you going to be showing videos? If the venue cannot provide these things, it will increase the cost of the event should you have to hire equipment from a specialist provider.

Make sure that your guests are dressed appropriately. See IDEA 20, Dressed to kill.

Try another idea...

Finally, look at the local area. Research how well the location is served by public transport. It is important that people who can't or don't want to drive should be able to find their way there. You could compile a list of local cab firms that you can make available to your guests; contact the companies in advance and you may be able to negotiate a special rate for trips to and from a railway station, for example. And if people are travelling a great distance, is there any convenient overnight accommodation? Important note: give your guests a range of options in different price categories as they may already be spending a lot of money on transport to the event, a new outfit and a gift.

One final point. Your choice of location can also be influenced by the time of year. Consider this scenario: a wedding held in an orangery in the height of summer is a lovely idea and the sun streaming through the windows will make it a truly glittering day. However the same setting in winter, with gloomy grey skies outside and the pitter-patter of rain on the glass, could prove to be a chilly affair.

Now find a location where you can match your list of your requirements to its facilities, and enjoy the party.

'Someone said that life is a party. You join in after it's started and leave before it's finished.'
ELSA MAXWELL, society hostess

Defining idea...

How did it go?

Q **I've an ideal venue but my guest list exceeds their capacity by ten. Is there anything I can do to encourage them to take the booking anyway?**

A *As I have mentioned, safety considerations mean that venues have to dictate numbers. I would suggest, however, that you might well have ten people who don't come. Not every single person you invited will be able to make it; no party ever has 100% attendance.*

Q **But how will I know for sure?**

A *Nothing in life is guaranteed. Make a provisional booking and then send out the invites pronto with an early RSVP date on them. Allow yourself at least two months' leeway in case you are the one person in a million to whom everyone says 'yes'.*

29

Under canvas

A marquee makes a versatile space in which to hold a party.

Remember 'Four Weddings and a Funeral'? For me the biggest star in part of the film is the fantastic marquee in which one of the weddings takes place.

Part of the charm of holding a party in a marquee is that it is easy for people to pop outside. Whether it is for a cigarette, a snog or some fresh air, clearly it will be less appealing to venture outside if it's pouring down with rain. And that is your first consideration. Are you prepared to run the risk of guests having to clamber across muddy grass? Will you be consumed with worry about the weather in the days running up to the party? Ready to take the risk? Then here's where to start.

Marquees are available in a wide range of shapes and sizes, both of which influence the price that you pay. Once you have set a date, shop around to see what is available to you – they can get booked up months in advance. You will need to show the marquee company the location that you intend to use to make sure that it is a suitable place for them to erect their tent. While marquees can be put up on

Here's an idea for you... **If you cannot find a chair colour that you like, look for a hire company with a respraying facility. While the chairs will be wooden and quite traditional in design, you can request a customised colour that will exactly match your requirements.**

sloping or uneven ground with the use of adjustable platforms or scaffolding, it will add to the overall cost.

Hiring a marquee is unlike booking a room in a hotel, where the floor is down, the walls are painted and the tables and chairs are in place. When you hire a marquee, you'll have to decide on all of these, which makes it more fun if you like to pick and mix before you make your decisions, and a bit of a challenge if you are clueless on colours and interior design. If you fall into the latter group, make sure that you run your choices by a friend or family member who is renowned for having good taste.

Now, here's the marquee checklist.

HOW LARGE A MARQUEE DO YOU NEED?

If you want to be generous allow approximately eight square feet per person for a buffet and fifteen square feet per person for a seated event. In addition to this you may need to allow for a dance floor, disco or band area. If it's a wedding you will also need a cake table and an area for guests to leave their gifts. You may also want to provide a corner for a coat check.

WILL YOUR GUESTS BE WARM ENOUGH WHATEVER THE WEATHER?

I would recommend, even at the height of summer, that you have heaters on hand especially if the event will run late into the night. Modern heaters throw out a vast amount of heat so you can be confident that if they are running no guest will feel a chill. You can also opt for a lining on the marquee to be doubly sure it will be warm.

You will probably need to prepare a seating plan in your marquee. See IDEA 48, *Side by side*, on how to approach this.

Try another idea...

CAN YOU HIRE EVERYTHING YOU NEED FROM ONE PLACE?

Yes, of course. I would discourage you from hiring a marquee from any company that cannot also provide all the seats, tables, lighting, etc., as it is important for the look of the event that everything is coordinated.

WHEN IS IT PUT UP AND TAKEN DOWN?

This is open to negotiation with the company but if your party is on a Saturday it will usually go up on the Thursday or Friday before, and it will be dismantled on the following Monday or Tuesday. If the marquee is up for several days, then you have to accept that the grass beneath will be damaged; make sure that whoever owns the land is aware of this.

STYLE GUIDE

Whatever the occasion you will want to coordinate the colours used throughout your marquee. If you are planning a wedding, you will aim for the interior to go with the bridesmaids' dresses or the wedding flowers.

'It always rains on tents. Rainstorms will travel thousands of miles, against prevailing winds, for the opportunity to rain on a tent.'
DAVE BARRY, US journalist

Defining idea...

If it is a ruby, silver or golden wedding anniversary, then you will be looking for these colours to dominate your scheme. This means choosing matching napkins and table linen and complementary tables and chairs. For the latter you will also need to consider the colour of the seat pad (and you can find anything from shocking pink to tartan at some companies) or, if you want the place to look really glamorous, chair covers. These neat fabric shifts, when dressed with bows or braids, transform plain chairs into dressy seats. And you must go and sit on the seats before you hire them; choose comfort over looks.

How did it go?

Q   I love the idea of a marquee for my birthday party but I am a winter baby. Is this wise?

A   There is something magical about walking through a dark night and entering a beautifully lit, fabulously decorated marquee. It is romantic in the true sense of the word, so go ahead. Make sure that you choose hard flooring (in place of matting, which is suitable for summer nights) and have plenty of powerful heaters. Then you'll be fine.

Q   But what if it is very windy?

A   Marquees are always properly anchored and once up are amazingly sturdy. (Let's be honest, the company that puts your marquee up wouldn't bother offering the service in winter unless they were sure it would stay in place.) In the UK, for example, they are made in accordance with EC safety standards and are manufactured to withstand wind loading of up to 60 mph. This is adequate for all but the fiercest of gales.

128

30

The class of glass

Reach for the perfect receptacle – present every drink in style.

It is absolutely fine, over a casual spaghetti dinner with friends, to serve up a glass of Italian red wine in a tumbler...

And if you are getting ready for a night on the town, then swigging beer from the bottle saves on washing up before you leave. However, if you are planning to entertain in style, then having just the right glass in which to serve up a drink should be high on your list of priorities.

HOW DO YOU CHOOSE THE RIGHT GLASS?

Are you serving champagne? Leave the glasses with a wide shallow bowl in the box. This design, the traditional champagne coupe, allows both the aroma and the bubbles to dissipate quickly, whereas the fizz will last that much longer in a tall slim flute. Champagne is best served in a narrow, straight-sided or tulip glass. Part of the appeal of this drink is the steady stream of bubbles rising up from the bottom of the glass and they get to travel that much further when there is some height to the drinking vessel.

Here's an idea for you... **Never overfill a wine glass. You want to pour the drink so that the glass is a third to half full at the most. This leaves room for the recipient to swirl the wine and tilt the glass to a 45° angle so that they can inhale the bouquet and enjoy the colour of the wine as they hold it up to the light.**

When it comes to selecting wine glasses, you should base your choice on form and function. Form, in that everyone likes different shapes and styles of stemware (while one person might favour cut glass, another will choose a clear bowl), and function in that the glass needs to enhance your enjoyment of the wine. What does that mean in design terms? Well, wine glasses with larger, broader bowls are perfect for red wines when you want to be able to inhale a bold bouquet. Those with smaller bowls and a narrower opening are ideal for enjoying the more delicate aromas of lighter white wines.

The scent of a wine is all important. So if you love to swirl your drink around in the bowl and dip in your nose to inhale the bouquet before you take your first sip, then make sure that you invest in a design that allows you to do this.

GLASSES FOR A DINNER PARTY

Are you planning to serve a different wine with every course? Then please, please, please have a different glass for each wine – if this is out of the question, then you will, really will, have to take empty glasses away from the table and rinse them between each wine. Position them on the table in order of use, from right to left so you will pour the drinks in the right order. (You'll note that if you are served correctly in any restaurant, the food will come from your left side and the wine from the right.) Don't forget to put a water glass on the table too. Even if people choose not to use it, if you wish to lay your table correctly, it should be there.

ANYONE FOR A COCKTAIL?

How much money do you want to spend here? You can add glass after glass after glass to your collection for serving cocktails but here are a few classics.

If you want to start mixing your own cocktails, go for IDEA 8, *The cocktail-hour kit*, and IDEA 9, *Stocking up*.

Try another idea...

- Martini: a classic triangular bowl design with a long stem which is also used for straight-up (without ice) cocktails such as Manhattans and Gimlets.
- Highball: a straight-sided design which is perfect for any drink that has a mixer, such as a whisky and soda, or a gin and tonic.
- Old-fashioned: also called a 'rocks' glass, these are short and round and come in small and large versions.
- Shot glass: a tiny piece of kit – only a few centimetres high – which is essential for enjoying good vodkas and tequilas.

Let's be realistic. You may invest in set after set of beautifully boxed, matching glasses but accidents do happen. It's inevitable that a glass will get broken and, over time, you'll end up with a collection that includes many different shapes and sizes. Here's my advice. Resist the temptation to put together your place settings with three glasses that match and one that does not. Use a random selection across the board. Have a solitary glass that doesn't match and it looks like you've made a mistake; vary shapes, sizes and colours and then, clearly, you are showing off your splendid collection!

Anyone for a drink?

'My grandmother is over eighty and still doesn't need glasses. Drinks right out of the bottle.'
HENRY YOUNGMAN, US comedian

Defining idea...

133

How did
it go?

Q   I much prefer to drink my wine from a short tumbler. Is there any reason why I should use a glass with a stem?

A   *I am in total sympathy with you. It is how I like to drink a wine I know, too. However, if you are not familiar with the wine, then this is no way to appreciate a new bottle. For a start, with your hand around the glass you are warming it up. This might be fine if it is a red wine, but is probably the last thing that you want to inflict on a good glass of white. A stem gives you something to hold on to without affecting the temperature of the liquid in the bowl.*

Q   Is that why brandy glasses always have a very short stem?

A   *Absolutely. Part of the pleasure of drinking brandy is to warm it in your hands to encourage the vapours to travel out of the glass and up your nose. (There should be a more delicate way to phrase that, but at least when it is said that literally, you know what I mean.)*

31

Bubbling over

**Life would be flat without the fizz of champagne; fun and
fancy celebrations call for a lively and sophisticated drink.**

Which is a perfect description of good
champagne.

Let's forget the lookalikes for now. I do not intend to deliver a list of brands and
vintages that you should buy; you ought to approach a specialist for that
information. But there is a lot of useful advice that I can share with you about
drinking champagne; I've made it a bit of a mission to get it absolutely right!

First things first, depending on your palate and whether you like things tart or
sweet, learn to recognise the following:
- Brut – very dry.
- Extra Sec – dry.
- Sec – slightly sweet.
- Demi-Sec – sweet.
- Doux – very sweet.

On to the practicalities.

THE BIG FREEZE

Never open a bottle until it has been chilled. Placing it in the fridge for two to four
hours should be sufficient. I have, on occasions, put champagne straight into the

Here's an idea for you...

If you are having a champagne party you may want to get a selection of the different sized bottles available. You can work out how much you need (based on five glasses per bottle) by knowing how many bottles make up the different sizes.

- Magnum – two bottles
- Jeroboam – four bottles
- Rehoboam – six bottles
- Methuselah – eight bottles
- Salmanazar – twelve bottles
- Balthazar – sixteen bottles
- Nebuchadnezzar – twenty bottles

freezer but experts will tell you that this is not a good idea so avoid it if you can; it taints the contents of the bottle. If you are in hurry then place the bottle in a bucket and surround it with a generous mix of ice and water. You can speed up the process by adding a handful of salt, which reduces the temperature of the ice. (I could give you the chemical equation for this process in order for you to check it out, but why not just trust me? It works.)

OPEN UP

Part of the reason that I have spent many years perfecting the art of enjoying champagne is that I spent many hours in hospital when I was younger, after opening a bottle and having the cork hit me straight in the eye. Partial blindness, however temporary a state, is terrifying: so years later, when I was ready to face my next bottle, I learned how to open it properly. Let's go.

Defining idea...

'Some people wanted champagne and caviar when they should have had beer and hot dogs.'
DWIGHT D. EISENHOWER

Before you begin, place a couple of glasses on a surface nearby so that you can catch any fizz that flows out of the bottle. Now, it's a simple process. Start by removing enough foil to expose the cork. Do not pull all of the foil away, as you may need this to give you a grip on the bottle. Point the champagne away from you (avoid anyone else in the room too), then slowly unwind the little wire handle on the side of the wire cage that covers the cork. Don't wrench it around if it doesn't come lose straight away. The more you agitate the bottle, the more likely you are to lose control of the cork. Once the cage has been removed, continue to keep a grip on the bottle while holding the cork with the other hand. Now slowly twist the bottle and ease out the cork.

The louder the pop when the cork is released, the fewer the bubbles you will have to enjoy when you drink it. You want the cork to be released with a whispered sigh, a gentle expulsion of the built-up gases which then allows you to pour the drink, rather than have it burst out of the bottle in a fountain of fizz. (Unless of course you have just won a Grand Prix, in which case the fizz fountain is exactly the effect you want.)

PERFECT POURING

Place your thumb in the dimple in the bottom of the bottle and allow your fingers to loosely grip the body. Use a clean napkin to wipe the rim of the bottle and then pour a small amount of champagne into each glass. Once that has settled, go back and top them up so that they are two-thirds full. (You can expect to get five glasses from a standard bottle.)

Try another idea...

If you have worked your way through a Jeroboam, see IDEA 16, *Ouch, ouch, ouch*, for some help the morning after.

Defining idea...

'Champagne, if you are seeking the truth, is better than a lie detector. It encourages a man to be expansive, even reckless, while lie detectors are only a challenge to tell lies successfully.'
GRAHAM GREENE

AND NOW THE FUN PART

The reason that champagne flutes have long stems is so that you can hold the glass by the stem and not by the bowl. The drink is served chilled and you don't want to warm it up. Now inhale the bouquet and take a sip. Champagne isn't a drink to swig and anyone who tells you otherwise probably refers to it as 'poo'.

Cheers!

How did it go?

Q   I would love to serve champagne all night at my party but my budget precludes this happening. Can I get away with serving sparkling wine instead?

A   *As long as you don't ask everyone else to bring champagne and provide none yourself, then it's fine to have sparkling wine. Buy a case of the real McCoy and supplement it with some good quality 'imitations'.*

Q   So how do I know what is good quality?

A   *As you are working to a budget, you should talk to a good wine merchant to see which he or she recommends as the best bottle for the price you want to pay. There are many different alternatives that will provide a fine fizz including Californian Cuvée Napa Mumm, Italian Asti and Spanish Cava.*

32

And the kids came too

At family parties or when you gather with friends, children are part and parcel of the group.

If you are taking your children to an event, you trust and pray that they won't embarrass you or cause a scene.

In another scenario, you have invited friends with children into your home and you expect them to behave in an appropriate way. So how can you avoid drama and conflict and ensure that the children behave like little angels throughout?

VISITING

It is important that children are prepared for an event. Tell them where they are going, when they are going and why – otherwise they could be confused or even scared, which is often the starting point for 'bad' behaviour. This briefing also gives you the chance to involve them in the event; if they are occupied, it reduces the opportunities for mishaps. So, if it is a wedding that you are taking them to, for example, you can promise that they can throw the confetti; at a Christmas party you might ask them to put the presents under the tree. Giving them these tasks, and emphasising how important it is that they perform them well, will help make children feel special and important.

Here's an idea for you...

Why not plan your party preparations so that the kids at the event have jobs to do? Draw up a list of suitable tasks that can be left until the last minute and when they arrive, give them a choice of what they would like to do. For example:

- **Empty the ice trays from the freezer into a bucket.**
- **Decorate the trifle.**
- **Fold the napkins.**
- **Put the sausages onto cocktail sticks.**
- **Take people's coats as they arrive and put them in the bedroom.**

Defining idea...

'**Childhood is a short season.**'
HELEN HAYES, actress

In the days before you head off to a gathering, make a point to mention good manners on every possible occasion. This could cover what they need to say to you if they wish to go to the toilet and you are having a conversation with someone; it might be how to behave at the dinner table. Think about some of the situations that may arise and explain how you expect them to behave:

- They are playing with other children in a home office – then it is bad manners to open the drawers on the desk.
- They are trying to find the bathroom but all the doors on a landing are closed – they should knock on a door and wait to see if they get a response before opening it and walking into the room.
- The food has been served and they want ketchup, which is out of their reach – they should ask someone to pass it rather than climb up on their chair and reach across.

These may all seem quite simple scenarios and if they were at home, they probably would be. But remember that in the middle of a party the excitement can be all consuming and they may act out of character.

PREPARING FOR CHILDREN TO ARRIVE

As the hostess, you can go a long way to making sure that children enjoy an event by putting certain things in place before they arrive. Kids get bored and when there are no distractions there can be plenty of opportunities for them to moan, so set aside a dedicated space where they can play safely. Provide board games, paints and crayons or a dressing-up box full of different outfits, which will keep them entertained for hours. You could provide a TV and video in another room and give them a choice of films to watch. (In order to avoid arguing about who makes the first selection, create a game out of getting them to pull numbers out of a hat. This should avoid cries of 'that's not fair!') And consider preparing a child-friendly meal and dessert. Set up a table where they can eat as a group. It's more fun for them and more relaxing for the grown-ups.

If you are planning a party for a child see IDEA 6, *Young at heart.*

Try another idea...

DEALING WITH CONFLICT

If a child gets upset, it's for a reason. However illogical the cause of their distress may seem to you, take them away from the situation and talk to them, cuddle them if they are in a state and if it's appropriate, and divert them by introducing a distraction. Leaving young children to look after themselves for too long is a recipe for disaster, so be aware of how long they are by themselves without adult supervision.

Last but most definitely not least, remember that children get tired. As a guest, however much fun you are having, be prepared to leave when it is clear that your children are worn out. As a host, make sure that there are beds available.

How did it go?

Q   I've read this chapter though I don't have kids of my own, but many of my friends do. It sounds very reasonable but what if I decide to have a party and don't want children there?

A   *That's a tricky one. Have you considered your friends' reaction? Parents are very protective and any slight might cause a rift in your relationship. Why is it that you don't want them there? Is it because you're worried that they will wreck your house? Relax. Your friends know you well enough to be aware that you are house-proud and won't let their children run riot.*

Q   I hear what you are saying. Fine, children are welcome but can I issue a list of dos and don'ts?

A   *With close friends, of course: but try and be reasonable. If you have included people on your guest list who do not know you very well, I would suggest that they might find this a little strange. The ideal solution to your dilemma would be to issue an invitation for drinks at 9 p.m. The people with children will either get a sitter or say 'no' to your party.*

33

Out and about

Organise an entertaining outing – it makes a welcome change to take people somewhere new.

Cast your mind back over your entertaining for the last few months; I bet it's predictable. How about doing something different?

How many times have you spent your Saturday cooking an impromptu lunch for friends that drift by, then spent the afternoon reading the weekend papers and finally wandered to your local bar for drinks where you stay until the end of the night? Now reflect on recent company events. Has the prospect of an open bar and drunken disco begun to pall?

How about a change? Read any listings guide for your home town (or beyond) and you'll find a host of different events are taking place. So get organised.

Here's an idea for you... **Why not go self-catering and take along a deluxe hamper to something like the races? Picnics are often allowed in specified areas (however, there may be a charge) and it makes a great way to start the day.**

MAKING THE CHOICE

Whether you choose a trip to the theatre, a day at the races, a game of paintball or a go-karting competition, you want everyone who comes along to enjoy the experience. The first rule of planning a group outing is to make a choice about where and when. Let's firstly address this on the understanding that you have friends or colleagues who are able to make a decision. Be democratic. Present everyone with three options, take a vote and once you know the result ignore any moaners.

Now approach it from another point of view. Much as you love and respect your friends and colleagues, you know they couldn't make an instant decision about anything (well, unless there was a substantial amount of money as a reward). In this situation, once you start to involve other people in the decision-making process you are lost; a homebody will suggest that it is too far to travel, a pessimist will predict that there might be rain. If this is an accurate description of those around you then present the group with a fait accompli: 'I am going to the races/theatre/a comedy club on Friday/Saturday/Sunday. Shall I get you a ticket?'

THE NEXT STEP

So what should you find out when you have democratically chosen the entertainment? Because there are so many different options, I am going to focus on my favourite outing – a day at the races. Here's a checklist using that as an example.

- Find out when the next meeting is taking place.
- Ask if there are discounts available to groups. It may be that for every twenty people who book, one person comes free. You may also receive a drinks voucher if you are not booking refreshments as part of the package.
- Is it worth booking an all-inclusive deal? These can be great value for money and add to the enjoyment of the day if several people in the party have never been before. It might include a behind the scenes tour and also someone who will answer all your questions about how to place a bet.
- Which enclosure should you choose? Depending on how much you pay you will be able to gain access to different areas and facilities. Tailor your choice according to whether you want to be able to go into certain bars or restaurants, the parade ring or the winners' enclosure. You might also want to make sure where seating is available if there are older people in the group.
- What type of refreshments are available? Do you need to make reservations at a restaurant in advance?

As the host of the event you have certain responsibilities. See IDEA 46, *The perfect host*, for some helpful tips.

Try another idea...

'*True happiness arises, in the first place, from the enjoyment of one's self, and in the next, from the friendship and conversation of a few select companions.*'
JOSEPH ADDISON, British politician and writer

Defining idea...

- Confirm the dress code. On certain race days, you will be expected to wear more formal attire.
- Check the facilities for children. For example, are there any special activities or entertainment?
- Where can you park? Is there a fee to pay? If you are travelling by public transport, is there a courtesy bus to the track?

PLANNING THE DAY

The chances are that you will be spending money in advance whatever you do. Depending on the nature of the trip, it could be on any of the following: entrance tickets, seat tickets, travel tickets, coach hire, car hire, maybe a deposit for refreshments. All of that adds up, so make sure that as soon as people decide they're coming on the trip, they pay their share. This also means that it is unlikely that you will have any 'no shows' on the day.

If you do your research thoroughly you'll have great day out, which everyone will enjoy – and remember.

Q **I've arranged the day and people need to stick to a very specific timetable if things are to run smoothly. What is the best way to impress the importance of this on everyone who is coming?**

How did it go?

A *Print up a timetable or schedule for everyone. If you are going to have to catch public transport then lie to your friends about what time the train/coach departs; I would recommend that a fifteen-minute safety margin is adequate. Include a dress code on the schedule. (There's a huge difference between an outfit for a day at the races and what people will choose to wear if they are going karting.) Also indicate when refreshments are going to be available so that no one sneaks off for a snack without realising that lunch is just around the corner.*

Q **What should I do if someone is late?**

A *Your responsibility is to the group. Stick to the original plan and leave it up to the tardy person to find their own way there.*

34

The price is right

Work to a budget – it is easier if you plan things properly. Can you put a price on fun? It would be lovely to be able to say 'no'...

However, the reality is that whatever entertainment you have in mind, you will have a finite amount of money that you can spend.

So how do you decide how much? Ask yourself the following questions:
- How much can I realistically afford?
- How many people am I going to be entertaining?
- What are my priorities?

These are essential, so let's address them.

Don't get carried away by thinking that the more you spend the better the time everyone will have. There is no point in throwing a huge party if you will be worrying for months afterwards about how you are going to clear your enormous credit card bill. In fact, you might start worrying well before the event, which is going to ruin the fun of planning the party and spoil your enjoyment of the whole occasion. Imagine being in a situation where you are mentally adding up the bill every time you see someone taking a drink or eating a canapé. It's just not worth it. So work within your means and don't allow yourself to be tempted.

Work out the maximum that you want to spend and then knock a small percentage off that figure. Mentally put that aside. There is bound to be something that you decide you need at the last minute and, that way, you can go and buy it – secure in the knowledge that you are still working within your budget.

Clearly the more people that you invite, the bigger the expense. You might be better off hosting an event for a few close friends – who will really value the time and effort that you have put into the occasion – rather than including many casual acquaintances who you are not really that bothered about seeing.

Do you want to impress your guests with delicious food, extravagant drinks or music supplied by an amazing DJ? Is it important to you that you hold the event in a particular type of location? Think about this so that you can apply some logic to your budget. Hiring a venue, inviting lots of people and choosing to use caterers and bar staff costs a lot of money. So maybe you should scale things down and host a party at home.

Right, now what will the money be spent on?

To answer this you need to make a comprehensive list of everything you need. Then you can allocate an amount to each item. The two most obvious elements are food and drink, but on top of these you might need to include decorations, for example candles or a Christmas tree. Then you need to consider whether you will need to hire glasses, extra chairs, china or cutlery – or will you buy a few extra pieces to supplement what you already have? It all adds up.

Defining idea...

'A budget tells us what we can't afford, but it doesn't keep us from buying it.'
WILLIAM FEATHER

150

The best way to stick to a budget is to work from a very detailed list. Stick to it and don't just add something to your shopping basket because it takes your fancy. The odd extra piece

See IDEA 27, *Make mine a double*, for some guidelines on the amount of drink to provide.

Try another idea...

of cheese, box of chocolates or packet of speciality coffee can make a big difference to the final food bill. If you are cooking, then detail each and every ingredient that you need to prepare the food.

Before you go to buy the drink, make a realistic calculation of how much the people that you have invited will actually consume. There's no reason to be mean with your allowance per person but, at the same time, you don't need to have the equivalent of a wine lake on tap. You can also figure in the fact that your guests will bring a bottle too – for most of them, this will be automatic.

The challenge with sticking to a budget is not to lose focus about where you want to spend your money. So keep a clear head, and you won't be counting the cost for months.

'We might come closer to balancing the Budget if all of us lived closer to the Commandments and the Golden Rule.'
RONALD REAGAN

Defining idea...

How did it go?

Q **My food bill looks pretty high. Any clues on where to economise?**

A *Well, it depends on what you are cooking. If you have planned three very exotic courses then maybe you could change one of the dishes for something a bit more basic. If there are a lot of ingredients to each recipe it will push up the cost, too.*

Q **Then is it better to have a simple starter or a simple dessert, the main course stays?**

A *It doesn't really matter. I would look in your cupboards and make a list of all the herbs, spices and assorted ingredients that you already have. Find a recipe that includes lots of these and then you won't have to buy so many things.*

Q **That's a nice idea but my kitchen isn't that well stocked so it isn't going to make a dramatic difference. Do you have another suggestion?**

A *Yes I do. Sometimes you have to look at a situation as a long-term project. Don't treat it as a 'once in a lifetime' event but embrace the idea that you are investing in the future. OK, right now you need to spend money on a range of ingredients, all of which are pushing up the cost, but I'm guessing that many of them will see you through three or four more dinners at the very least. This time around you may need to buy a jar of honey, some dried herbs and a bag of flour – but if you store them correctly then next time there'll be three items less in your trolley at the checkout.*

35

All by myself

Have the confidence to arrive at an event without a date.

So you are single. And you know that you are going to be walking into a sea of couples when you arrive at the party...here's how to deal with it.

Even if friends, work colleagues or family are also on the guest list, it can still be a daunting prospect.

The reason that you are going out is because you want to enjoy yourself. If you are nervous, uncomfortable and stressed, that is just not going to happen. Ooze confidence, feel at ease and appear relaxed – and you will be in the mood to party all night. How do you achieve that state of mind? By preparing yourself both physically and mentally in the hours before you leave your home.

PREPARATION

Plan your day so that you have plenty of time to get dressed. If you wait until the last minute to choose your outfit, you may just grab something in a panic that you regret wearing later on. This is not the time to dress in brand new clothes. When you try something on in a shop, you will only be wearing it for a matter of minutes.

Here's an idea for you...

Make an appointment with your beautician or hairdresser or barber on the day of the party. Have your hair trimmed, nails manicured (that goes for both sexes), eyebrows neatened (that goes for both sexes too) or legs waxed (just the women...). You will feel much more confident if you know that you are looking your best.

Don it for a party and it has to survive several hours. During this time you might discover that the collar is actually tighter than you realised or that the waistband digs into your side. Bearing in mind the dress code – and make sure that you double check that with the host – pick something that you are comfortable wearing. That way you'll know that the straps on a top will not slip down your arms or that a zip won't mysteriously get stuck. Choose shoes that have seen their fair share of action.

PRACTICAL MATTERS

You want to be able to make conversation, so think ahead about the kind of people that you are likely to encounter. Is there a common interest that presents a natural starting point for discussion? Watch the news or read a paper in the hours before you go out. Everyone will have an opinion on a hot political scandal, for example, so you will be able to engage in conversation if you are up to speed. Time your arrival so that plenty of people are already at the event, but don't leave it so late that cliques have already formed. It takes time for everyone to relax and start to mingle at an event, whether they are there with a partner or not.

BODY LANGUAGE

Make a point of obtaining a drink as quickly as possible. Catch the eye of a waiter if drinks are being circulated on trays or head for the bar so that you get a glass in your hand. It doesn't need to be alcoholic; a refreshing fruit juice might be just what you need. This is important because it gives you something to do with your hands and, if you are nervous, you will be less likely to fidget with your clothes or your bag.

Do you arrive at family parties alone and get an endless stream of questions about your single status? See IDEA 51, *Family fun*, on how to deal with stress at such gatherings.

Try another idea...

Don't stare down at the floor or up to the ceiling. Let your eyes drift across the room so that you can make eye contact with someone and initiate a conversation. (Practise your smile beforehand – you do not want to look like a grinning idiot, but you do want to appear friendly and approachable.)

TALKING POINTS

Don't be afraid to initiate conversations. You may want to brush-up on your small talk before you go to the event so that you feel comfortable approaching other people. One of the easiest ways to start a dialogue is with a question such as, 'Are you a friend of the bride or groom?' or 'Have you seen the band that is setting up. Aren't their outfits amazing?' or even 'Did you know that the managing director was going to be making a speech?' By starting a conversation like this you provide an easy opening for the other person to respond; it also gives you a chance to develop your listening skills and people respond to a good listener. Always resist the temptation to jump in before the other person has finished speaking. It suggests that you consider your point of view as more important than his or hers – no one responds well to that approach.

'A conversation is a dialogue, not a monologue. That's why there are so few good conversations: due to scarcity, two intelligent talkers seldom meet.'
TRUMAN CAPOTE

Defining idea...

Circulate in the room, make conversations and you won't be spending too much time alone. And don't forget to enjoy yourself!

How did it go?

Q **I have tried to overcome my fear of arriving alone, but despite following your advice, I still dread it.**

A *The more that you dwell on the situation beforehand the more you will build it up in your head as something to be endured, not enjoyed. Part of the reason that I suggest going to a beautician on the day, for example, is that if you are nervous it gives you something to occupy your time in the hours before the event. When you are well prepared you really have nothing to worry about.*

Q **Fine, but I do worry about getting stuck talking to someone and not being able to make an escape. Surely I'm not alone?**

A *No, you're not! It can be tricky but the solution is really simple. All you need to do is wait for a lull in the conversation and offer your hand to be shaken while you say, 'It's been lovely to meet you, but I need to go and find the cloakroom, please excuse me.' Turn and walk away, and you're free.*

36

'Here's looking at you, kid...'

Learn the art of making a toast, whether it's a planned or spontaneous gesture.

I know the line. Like many others, I have probably watched Humphrey Bogart deliver it a thousand times in 'Casablanca' and yet it never ever fails to send a shiver of anticipation down my spine.

Could there be a more romantic gesture than someone looking across the room, raising a glass in your direction, meeting your eyes and then delivering a toast in your honour? I'm fairly sure if a man had the right tone, the right looks and the right delivery that I would be putty in his hands. Dream on....

Reality bites. So while I wait for that life-changing moment (I know that I shouldn't hold my breath), here's how it happens in the more everyday world.

Most toasts are part of a planned celebration and follow a tradition that has been in place for years. In these situations, you will already know that you are expected to make a toast and you'll be aware of the kind of event in which you are participating. If you are not clear about any of this, then here's a checklist:

157

Here's an idea for you... **If you are struggling with the words to open your toast, why not use a quote from, or story about, a famous individual who has been in the same situation? Here are a couple of examples. If you are toasting an individual on a sporting achievement, find a quote from someone who won Wimbledon several times. If it is to mark an achievement in business, find a quote from a successful entrepreneur.**

When somebody asks you to make a toast...

- Know the specifics of the event. Is it formal? Is it a family party? Will everyone present know you?
- Be aware of who you are talking about. Is the toast to honour one person or a couple?
- Find out the reason. Is it to mark a specific milestone such as a birthday or a wedding anniversary? Is it to mark an achievement such as winning a competition or coordinating a community project successfully?
- Look the part. Is there a dress code at the event?

There's potential for upsetting people here, so make sure you do your preparation and get it right; clear up all those details.

Now you've done that, here's the right approach.

- Be sure of what you are going to say and rehearse beforehand. If you can think of one, a witty one-liner at the start will put people in the right mood to have a swig. Avoid in-jokes that only you and a select few at the gathering will understand.
- Aim to keep it reasonably short. The words that accompany a toast should be spoken in less than five minutes from start to finish. (Making a speech is a completely different issue and you're not there to do that.)
- Put everything in context. How much information do you need to give as part of the toast so that everyone present knows the reason for raising their glass?

And don't forget: in order for people to share in a toast they must have something in their glass to drink. Make sure that someone, whether the waiting staff at a catered event or yourself at a small gathering, has circulated the champagne or topped up glasses with wine before you start to speak.

If you have been asked to make a speech, you'll find help at IDEA 4, *Can you hear me at the back?*

Try another idea…

The body language of someone making a toast is incredibly important. You need to face in the direction of the person whom you are toasting. And you must do it with a smile on your face; a touch of deference is in order if the recipient is considerably older than you and a touch of self-deprecating humour – a touch – is appropriate if they are from your generation.

Raise your glass to the person and look at them as you make the toast. Once you have finished speaking, tip your glass towards the person that you are honouring. If they are within arm's length of you, then it is appropriate at that point to clink their glass. Then take a sip of your drink.

On certain occasions you will be one of several people who are going to stand up and speak. You final duty in these situations is to pass on the 'speech baton' to the next person in line. Once your toast is completed then turn your body so that you are facing in their direction. Use one of the following phrases: 'It is now my pleasure…', 'I am very happy to turn the floor over to…' or 'You will be delighted when I introduce…'. Then get out of the limelight. It's someone else's turn to take the heat.

'The wise ones fashioned speech with their thought, sifting it as grain is sifted through a sieve.'
THE BUDDHA

Defining idea…

Now raise your glass…

How did
it go?

Q **I am all set for the big event but I am not sure how I can guarantee that everyone has a drink. We are not having waiting staff and I can't be in two places at once. I am supposed to be sitting at the top table, so surely if I suddenly disappear, the recipient will know something is up?**

A *You need help. In this case, brief someone at every other table in the room that you will be making a toast either at a specific time or after a specific course – just after everyone has collected a cup from the coffee station would be appropriate. Ask those people to make sure that everyone who is sitting at their table has a drink at that point.*

Q **That's sorted. Just to check, are there any subjects that I should avoid?**

A *Yes, don't talk about sex or money. Also the toast isn't about you so avoid any personal life stories. If, when you rehearse, you realise that you are saying 'I' quite frequently, then you need to rewrite the toast.*

37

Party games for kids

Organised fun keeps kids content – here's how to have harmony with a bit of planning.

Trivial Pursuit and Monopoly, Risk and Cluedo, these classics appear time after time at gatherings. It's easy to entertain people when you can reach for a board game.

But what do you do if you have nothing like this in the toy box? You want to achieve the following:

- keep the kids happy
- get everyone get involved
- not take hours setting things up, and
- not spend a lot of money!

Right, let's address some basics. What's the profile of the group? For example, are we taking about very young children or do you have to entertain a group of teenagers (now, there's a challenge)? Here are some ideas.

Here's an idea for you...

If the ages of the children are quite mixed, try and find games where you match up one teenager and one younger child. Quite a good one is Newspaper Fashion, where you give each pair a pile of newspapers, sticky tape and coloured pens. They then have ten minutes to design an outfit that one of the two must wear. It usually works best if the older one in the group dresses up the younger, but let them make their own decision about this. The game ends with a fashion parade in front of one or two assembled adults with a prize going to the pair whose outfit either stays on the longest or which everyone agrees looks the best.

YOUNG CHILDREN

The most important thing to bear in mind with young children is that no game should go on for too long. Keep them to about twenty minutes for maximum fun, without having so much time that conflicts will develop.

If you have plenty of room how about Balloon Keepy-uppy? Divide the children into two teams and put them on either side of a net (or a line of some kind). Allow each team four touches of the balloon before they must get it over to the other side. As soon as the balloon hits the ground or is touched more than four times, then the last child to touch it has to retire. Continue until there is only one person left standing.

If you are tight on space try the Memory Game. Take a mixture of different household objects with unusual shapes (a biscuit cutter and a toothbrush, for example). Now blindfold one child and hand them something from the bag. If they guess the object then hand them another, if not then show them the item and they are out. Pass on to the next person. Keep going until there is only one person left. This game has the advantage of keeping the kids sitting still, so it is a good one to play after they have been playing something very boisterous like Musical Bumps.

Looking for games for grown-ups? See IDEA 40, *Adult games*.

Try another idea...

YOUNG TEENS

As a group that can notoriously become bored (and very vocal about it), you'll want to find games that will appeal to their more obnoxious tendencies. Killer is a classic but works on two levels. The first is that someone gets to be a murderer; the second is that you can award a special prize for the person who acts out the best death scene. For anyone who hasn't played it: count how many people are playing and cut some paper into a corresponding number of pieces. Mark one with an X (indicating the killer), fold them all up and put them in a bag. Ask everyone to pick out a piece and then sit in a circle around a table or on the floor. Everyone has to look at the other people's faces and the killer has to take the opportunity – when they don't think that they are being watched – to wink at someone and thereby 'kill' that person. The victim has to 'die', preferably horribly. If another player thinks he or she knows the killer's identity, they can say, 'I know the murderer' and then name their suspect. If they get it right then they have won; get it wrong and they too are condemned.

Here's another game to appeal to teenagers' dark side: Egg Head. You have to do some advance preparation here. Count the number of

'You can't win unless you learn how to lose.'
KAREEM ABDUL-JABBAR, US basketball player

Defining idea...

163

people who will be playing and hard boil that number of eggs. Place a large tablecloth (or plastic sheet if you are very house-proud) over the table. Ask everyone to sit down. Put all of the eggs in a bowl, adding one fresh egg somewhere in the pile. Now get everyone to roll a dice; the lowest number goes first. They turn to the person on their left or right and say 'Pick me an egg, egghead'. An egg is picked from the bowl – it must be the first one that they touch – and passed to the person who has made the request. They then, in one smooth action, have to break the egg in one smashing motion against their forehead. There's no need to explain who loses.

How did it go?

Q   **Well, the kids seemed to enjoy the egg game, but I wasn't prepared for the mess. What else should I have done?**

A   *Sorry, that was my fault. In addition to the tablecloth or plastic sheet, you do need to have a damp cloth and a tea towel or absorbent kitchen roll to hand. This is to mop up the individual who got egg on their face, and also to clear up any egg that hit the floor before it can soak in and stain.*

Q   **So now I have a lot of hard-boiled eggs sitting around. Should I make egg and cress sandwiches?**

A   *Are you mad? Do you know how mucky kids' hands can be even before they have been charging around at a party for a while? Gather all the bits together and bin them. Now.*

38

At the last minute

Entertaining for the time-challenged person.

Surprise, surprise... some friends have just rung to say that they are in your area and would love to stop by.

How delightful, how inconvenient, how the hell are you going to be able to entertain them with just an hour to get your house straight, give yourself a wash and brush up and have some food available should they decide to stay on?

Panic now and all is lost. You will be wasting precious minutes which could be used much more constructively.

My first piece of advice is to prioritise. If the house is a tip, a quick clean up is essential; if there is a dish in the freezer, which you can take out to defrost, do this now. If you are going to put together a few appetisers from scratch, now is the time to check the fridge, the cupboards and the vegetable rack and start to think about which snacks can be quickly assembled. As for your appearance – could questions be asked about your personal hygiene? You are going to have to fit in a quick shower before they arrive. Now here's how.

Here's an idea for you... **When you answer the phone and someone suggests dropping in at the last minute, stall them. If they say that they will be free in an hour, then respond that it would lovely to see them but you have to run an errand and will only be back in two. That should give you ample time to sort everything out.**

HOUSE-PROUD

Decide in which areas you are going to entertain. Go round these rooms with a big bin bag and fill it with anything that isn't breakable but that needs to be cleared away, such as newspapers and magazines, half-done homework or stray items of clothing. Put the bag in the bottom of your wardrobe – you can sort it out once your guests have gone.

Now wipe down any surfaces that show ring marks or are very dusty. Work through every room (except the bathroom, but I'll come to that later). Lastly, run a vacuum cleaner across the floor. Remember to clean up any area through which your guests might pass: the hall, corridors and landings that lead to the bathroom are probably on the list. Check for anything that is very dirty. It is easier to remove a rug that is covered with dog hairs or a candle that is coated in candle wax than to try and clean them up in the valuable minutes that are available to you. Light a scented candle; an appealing smell will always detract from a few minor horrors. If your friends are arriving at dusk or later, dim the lights. This can help to hide a multitude of sins.

LOOKING GOOD

Once you have finished your clean up, jump in the shower. Make sure that you use a scented shampoo or body wash, as the aroma from this will linger and leave the bathroom smelling wonderful long after you have finished in there. While you are in the bathroom use the opportunity to tidy it and give it a quick wash and brush up too. Put clean towels in there, so use the existing ones to wipe down all surfaces, including mirrors. Throw any messy bottles, gunked-up tubes of toothpaste or half-used toilet rolls into a carrier bag (making sure that the tops are firmly on the bottles) and again, hide it in the bottom of your wardrobe. Put in a fresh toilet roll and clean fluffy towels. Dress in an outfit in which you feel comfortable but know that you look good. If you are going to pull on jeans, then team them with a slightly dressy top.

If you are the kind of person that entertains at home on a regular basis, see IDEA 10, _Prepare to party._

Try another idea...

SNEAKY TREATS

I know I will sound smug if I tell you this, but I am going to share my secret with you anyway. I keep partially cooked French loaves in the freezer; you can buy them from any supermarket and they are perfect for emergencies. I always have a couple of bags of tortilla chips and jars of salsa tucked away at the back of the cupboard. When I use up my supply of tinned tuna and chopped tomatoes I always replace them instantly. How does this help with last minute entertaining? Here's how…

You can empty the tortilla chips out of a bag and into a beautiful bowl in seconds. You can decant the salsa from the jar and into a stylish dipping bowl in minutes. It doesn't take long to mix tuna with mayonnaise and put it next to a glass filled with breadsticks for a quick treat.

Now, if you have time, put on the kettle or open a bottle of wine and sit down in the lounge. When your guests arrive you will look amazingly relaxed.

'Time is nature's way of keeping everything from happening at once.'
WOODY ALLEN

Defining idea...

167

How did
it go?

Q   You were right; I did think you were smug when you talked about having food ready for emergencies! I got the rest, but what do you use your tin of chopped tomatoes for?

A   *That's for the French bread; sorry, I should have explained. It's for crostini, little pieces of bread served with a topping, that make a great appetiser or instant canapé.*

Q   OK. What do you do with them?

A   *Sorry. Grab the bread from the freezer and cook it according to the manufacturer's instructions. While it is in the oven, open the tin of tomatoes. Get some olive oil and pour a little into a saucer. When the bread is cooked, cut it into slices and then dip the top of each slice into the oil. Now scoop a small amount of chopped tomato on to the top of each piece. Put these under a medium grill for only a minute and serve.*

39

Room to party

It's time to move your furniture and set up your home for entertaining.

Take a look around your house. If you have invited people for drinks, dinner or a night of dancing, have you given any thought to how they will fit in?

Fit in physically, that is. Have you considered whether the area needed for the number of people you've invited far exceeds the space available to you? If this has got you thinking about your guest list, then good. While describing a party as a 'crush' might mean it was a great success in some circles, I prefer to know that my guests can get to the kitchen for a drink, find their way to the buffet table for a snack and have a reasonably short wait for the bathroom.

Let's take this last point under consideration. Unless you have a downstairs cloakroom and a bathroom upstairs, you can expect queues to form when there is a crowd of people drinking in the house. How do you address this?

Here's an idea for you... **If you don't have any storage space and are on good terms with your neighbours then enlist their help. If they are coming to the party, all the better. Ask them if you can store one or two pieces of furniture in their house overnight and not only can you rely on their help with moving the pieces out, but you can be pretty sure, if they have enjoyed the event, that they will help you restore order the next day.**

Start by making sure that the area next to the bathroom is clear of clutter. Is there a side table on your landing that could be moved to another location? It might make a useful extra surface downstairs, in the corner of the lounge, for example – so that people have somewhere to put their drinks, or in order to provide you with somewhere to put a selection of nibbles. Is there a bedroom next door to the bathroom? When people get bored of standing in a queue, they look for the first available place in which to sit down. Make sure that this room is tidy but also consider grouping a couple of extra chairs in an empty corner. If there is not already a mirror in there, do you have a floor-standing one that you could move into the room just for the night? This means women can check their make-up and hair before or after they have visited the bathroom – freeing that up in record time... I'm not being sexist, but women do tend to spend longer in there.

Now, what about the rest of your rooms?

Let's start in the hallway. Stand at the front door and look in. Imagine that six people arrive at the same time. Are there any pieces of furniture in the area that could be removed, thus making more space available when people come through the front door? Discount the umbrella stand and the coat rack in the winter, as these will be needed for wet or snow-soaked gear. Remove anything that isn't nailed down!

Clearing up after a party needs a little organisation. For some helpful advice see IDEA 19, _It's a messy business..._

Try another idea...

Now walk to the lounge. How many sofas or armchairs do you have in the room? Have you put in a beanbag? Then please remove it and place it somewhere out of the way. Is there more than one coffee table conveniently positioned in front of a group of seats? Leave one in place and move the rest upstairs, or store them in the garage overnight, in order to free up more floor space. The last thing that you want to do is leave the place looking empty and bereft of interest; but you do want to allow plenty of room for people to move around and socialise.

Lastly consider the kitchen, and here you have a dilemma. The table needs to stay but how many chairs should be left in place too? You know your friends. If they are likely to congregate in the kitchen than leave the seats in place so that they can gossip in comfort.

Think about all the furniture in your home and ask yourself if it will be used at the party. If the answer is no, then clear it out.

'I have been black and blue in some spot, somewhere, almost all my life from too intimate contacts with my own furniture.'
FRANK LLOYD WRIGHT

Defining idea...

How did
it go? **Q** **I have realised that by removing all of the excess furniture I don't
actually want it back. Now what?**

    A *That's great news, there is nothing better than a good decluttering session
to clear up your home and make life a whole lot simpler. I guess it depends
on where you have stored all the excess. Why not ask around among your
friends and see if anyone needs a new table/chair/sofa/lamp?*

    Q **Actually it is in my neighbours' garage. They came to the party;
can I use this as a bartering tool?**

    A *If you mean what I think you mean, then no way. ('I showed you a good
time so you owe me a favour': that would be very rude.) Grab a bottle of
wine (not a horrible one, but that nice vintage that you tucked away just in
case it was needed at the end of the night, only it never was) and pop next
door. Present them with the bottle and thank them for storing the furniture.
Then ask if they can keep it until the following weekend, by which time you
will have hired a van, found the details of a local auction house or junk
shop and arranged to deliver all the furniture there.*

40

Adult games

Parties provide the perfect excuse for a little organised fun and grown-ups rarely get the chance to behave like children...

Which is probably a good thing. But given the opportunity to take part in a game, most people will exhibit childlike glee at the chance to form a team and try to beat the opposition.

But can I now add a note of caution? If someone is very competitive when they're sober, then there's a chance that they may become overly competitive, to the point of aggression, when they've had a drink. This doesn't necessarily follow, but you could do worse than to bear it in mind.

On with the fun.

How well do you know the people that are going to be playing the games? And are they all acquainted? This will influence the type of game you suggest. If, for example, they are all old school or college friends, then a game involving physical contact should present no problem. Alternatively, when several people are, at best, known to each other just by sight or reputation, then consider a non-contact icebreaker as the first game that you play.

Here's an idea for you...

Why not arrange to have a game evening at your house? Ring round your friends and find out which board games they own. Then ask each person to bring a different one. Set up tables in various places, labelling each one with a number. Now give a number to each game and when people arrive give them a piece of paper that has one of those numbers written on it. Send them to the appropriate table and let the games commence.

ICEBREAKERS

Icebreakers are designed to help everyone present get to know each other. The idea is that people will find out each other's names and get to feel comfortable within the group. Keep them quite basic; if anyone is feeling nervous then the last thing you want to do is give them a whole list of rules that they need to memorise and follow. It will only add to their discomfort if they get part of the game wrong when everyone else seems to have grasped the idea with ease.

One of the best examples of an icebreaker is the Celebrity Game. List the names of various well-known personalities on 'stickies' (you know, the notepads with the little adhesive strip at the top). As people enter the room, stick one of these to their foreheads – do warn them that this is what you are planning to do before slapping it on otherwise they might be inclined to leap back in alarm. Now they have to go around the room, taking it in turns to ask and answer a question (only one per person, so that people circulate) until they have guessed their identity correctly. Tell them that they are only allowed to ask questions that have a straight 'yes' or 'no' answer and make a point of loudly drawing attention to anyone who cheats. It's all part of the fun.

Defining idea...

'Games lubricate the body and the mind.'
BENJAMIN FRANKLIN

GRASP A GLASS

If you are single and asked to a party, see IDEA 35, *All by myself*, for some advice.

Try another idea...

If everyone is of legal drinking age, you can have a lot of fun with drinking games. Be responsible about this, and draw the line when it is clear that anyone has consumed a little too much. You hope to be able to trust adults to know their limits, but not everyone is that self-aware.

If you are planning a night out with a group of people, then take along a dice. Tell everyone to be there right on time and then produce the dice. Take it in turns to roll it. The first person who rolls a six gets to nominate a drink. (I would suggest that you stick to simple and straightforward drinks rather than let people suggest revolting mixtures.) The second person to roll a six has to pay for the drink and the third person to roll a six has to drink it. This is not a bad way to start the evening if some of the people in the group do not know each other that well, as people will be eagerly observing each person's roll of the dice and expressions of sympathy or congratulations will be offered depending on the outcome of each throw. You might only play two or three rounds, before you put away the dice and resume 'normal' drinking patterns, but it's fun for a while.

Games are a great way to involve everyone in a group. Use your judgement on just how rowdy they should be.

'Games are a compromise between intimacy and keeping intimacy away.'
ERIC BERNE, writer

Defining idea...

175

How did
it go?

Q   I like the idea of the dice game, but I don't trust my friends to choose the drinks. Do you have another suggestion?

A   *Yep. Place your Bets is a dice game that allows you to choose your own poison. How much of it you have to consume is a different matter but the good thing about this game is that people who are not big drinkers can have a white wine spritzer, regularly topped up with soda water, without feeling that they are being party poopers. Here's how to play it. Someone says 'place your bets'. You decide what number you think they will roll and put that number of fingers on top of the table. Tuck the rest under your hand and if you think they will throw a six then make a fist and place it on the table. Then the person rolls the dice. If you predicted the right number, you are in the clear. If you got it wrong, then you have a drink: take the same number of sips as the number on the dice.*

Q   How do you decide who gets to roll the dice?

A   *Start by everyone having a go and whoever rolls the highest (or lowest) number is the first caller. The dice is then passed clockwise around the group.*

41

It's all in the decoration

Set the scene for your party by dressing up your space.

Whether you have invited people into your home, or are hosting an event at a restaurant, club or bar, it is almost certain that you will want to embellish the existing decor.

In both cases be realistic about what you can achieve. Consider your budget, work out how much time you will have to decorate and be honest with yourself about how much help you can expect from other people on the day.

If there is a theme to the party then creating an appropriate look is part and parcel of the whole affair. You might achieve a mood with simple details, giving a subtle nod to the theme of the affair without going over the top. Alternatively you may want to make an out-and-out statement, which leaves no one in any doubt of why they are there.

Here's an idea for you...

When you are recruiting, carry around with you a really large and imposing looking notebook. The minute someone agrees to help out with the preparations, ask them if they have any particular skills and then allocate them a specific task. Place the notebook on a surface nearby, open it up to a blank page and be sure that they watch you while you make a note like this: 'New Year's Eve – Jo will be helping to wash and polish all of the champagne glasses.' Write their phone number (mobile as well) next to the note. Now they have no choice. If they want to come to the party, but fail to turn up to wash the glasses, there is a chance that they will not have anything to drink champagne out of on New Year's Eve. I guarantee that the majority of people will fall for this even if you yourself know that you would just get on and sort out the glassware regardless!

MONEY – CONSIDER YOUR BUDGET...

Whatever the theme, the first step is to make a list of all the decorative items that will reflect the overall theme of the party. Let's take a particular theme as an example. How about a Hawaiian Luau? Here's what you will need to budget for:

- Hula skirts.
- Lei.
- Palm trees (that would be the blow-up ones).
- Macaws or parrots (they might be fluffy toys or inflatables).
- Exotic flower displays.
- Pineapples.
- Colourful flying fish (again, probably not the real things!).

Now all of that adds up. Imagine you are making a list for a *Star Wars* party, a Gangsters and Molls fancy dress do or a Spanish fiesta: in each case there is a whole host of props that could be used to dress up the room.

TIME – WORK OUT HOW MUCH YOU WILL HAVE

Need some tips for clearing up after the party? See IDEA 19, *It's a messy business...*

Try another idea...

It's all very well to have a vision in your mind of a recreation of a scene from *Blue Hawaii...* In fact it's not simply all very well, it's a fantastic idea. And if you could build into your budget an Elvis impersonator, that would be brilliant. Could you also set up a paddling pool in the room and have some sand delivered to mimic a beach? Sorry, I got a little carried away there with the whole idea – back to the matter in hand, timing.

Here's the thing. It takes a lot longer than you think to blow up a hundred balloons. And there is more to draping streamers across the ceiling then just grabbing a length of paper and a few drawing pins and throwing them up at random.

Depending on the nature of the occasion, consider the following points:
- If you are having a buffet table, you will need to dress this up appropriately.
- If you expect the party to spill into the garden, then you should allow yourself time to put up fairy lights and stake out garden flares.
- If it is Halloween, how quickly can you carve a pumpkin? Bear in mind that you will be working with a very sharp knife and that this is not something that you want to rush!
- If it is St Patrick's Day, how long are you going to spend trying to dye tablecloths and napkins emerald green?

'God loves to help him who strives to help himself.'
AESCHYLUS

Defining idea...

179

Defining idea...

'Small projects need much more help than great.'

DANTE

ASSISTANCE: BE HONEST ABOUT HOW MUCH HELP YOU CAN EXPECT

People are always happy to volunteer to help out, when the date of the party is in the dim and distant future. I'll lay good money on the chance that if ten people volunteer, only five of them will actually deliver the goods on the day – so don't be unrealistic about what it is possible to achieve with a smaller than expected group of helpers.

How did it go?

Q   You don't seem to place much faith in people's promises. Are you sure that you are not being unfair?

A   Yes, absolutely positive. Lots of personal experience has proved that you will get, at the very best, half of your helpers turning up as planned.

Q   So should I just ask double the amount of people than I need?

A   I think that is a great suggestion. If all of your friends or work colleagues remain true to their word, then you will have the job done in half the time, which gives you the chance to have a long luxurious soak in the bath, rather than a quick shower and brush up.

42

Tools of the trade

Just what kit do you need to invest in for regular entertaining?

It is always possible to make do. So please don't start to read this and begin to feel inadequate!

And don't think that you need to rush out to the shops and spend a fortune. That would be the very worst thing that you could do, because part of the pleasure of putting together all of the bits and pieces that you may use while entertaining is collecting them over a period of time.

It has taken me years to pull together the various accoutrements that might be viewed as essential: gorgeous red wine glasses from my wedding list, pasta dishes from a shop specialising in white china seconds, table linen found while rummaging around at a sale – the list goes on, but you get my point. Get hold of pieces from different places and build up your collection over the years and it has a great deal more value to you than a bulk buy at Ikea.

So, what should be on the list?

Here's an idea for you... **Make a list of all of the items that you would like to have, and find specialist suppliers for them. Keep a note of the company name, number and website and when your birthday or Christmas is approaching, pass on the details to people who will be buying you a gift. It saves them searching for a present and guessing – and in appreciation, you can cook them a meal at which their gift will be put to good use.**

Let's start with the requirements for a dinner party when you will be serving a starter, main course and pudding:

- Starter plate or soup bowl (with knife and spoon).
- Dinner plate
- Dessert bowl/plate
- Bread and butter plate (with knife).
- Napkin.
- Knife.
- Fork for main course, plus a dessert fork.
- Dessert spoon.
- Red and white wine glasses and water glass.

That's the basics. When considering your cutlery you might also want to include fish knives, steaks knives and tea and coffee spoons.

Then there's the possibility of more personal pieces. I would suggest that a fair proportion of the items that you buy would reflect your signature dishes – those tried and tested recipes that always work – and your favourite type of food.

For example, I like to serve Italian food. A dinner will start with an avocado, mozzarella and tomato salad followed by spaghetti carbonara with garlic bread and finish with a Sarah Lee pecan Danish pastry (I firmly believe this to be the best dessert in the entire world, transcending all cultural barriers!). This means that I have a huge white platter for the starter, dishes for the pasta, a wooden plate for the bread and tiny plates for the dessert, because it is very rich. This meal also requires something to serve the salad and pasta with.

IDEA 30, *The class of glass,* gives a guide to a range of glassware that will mean you can serve every drink in style.

Try another idea...

You see what I mean? If you regularly serve seafood, you'll need some lobster forks, oyster knives and crab crackers. Maybe you cook a lot of Chinese food or Mexican dishes? Then you'll need the kit to match the meal. Now for some designer details. What else is there to consider?

Think about the elements of a well-dressed table. It may include the following:
- A floral display, so you need a range of vases.
- Candlelight: collect different candlesticks and tea light holders.
- Neatly placed napkins, which are rolled up into stylish napkin rings.
- Place names: hand-written cards, standing upright in small holders.
- A water jug, but make sure that it pours cleanly and doesn't dribble or drip.
- Wine coasters, onto which the bottles are placed.

'I have measured out my life with coffee spoons...'
T.S. ELIOT

Defining idea...

Now think about other types of food that you might serve. Does the menu include any of the following?
- Corn on the cob – you will need corn holders.
- Pie or quiche – then a pie server is essential; try serving a slice with a knife and see how much mess you can make...
- Pizza – cutting it at the table is much more flamboyant than bringing out slices, so you'll want a good pizza wheel.

Defining idea...

'All that changing of plates and flapping of napkins while you wait forty minutes for your food.'
HUGH CASSON, British architect

There is no doubt that once you start to entertain on a regular basis you will want to have all the 'right' accoutrements. I don't consider money the issue (as in 'I can't afford to go out and buy all these pieces right now') – as I have previously said, it's more fun to collect them over time. One last source of inspiration is to be conscious of all the different ways that your food is served when you eat at different restaurants. I'm not suggesting that you take a photograph of the place settings when you arrive (although if you have a camera phone and are obsessive about details then this might work for you), it's more about making a mental note of different shaped dishes or unusual accessories that a specialist restaurant will use.

I could continue ad infinitum but I hope that has given you a good idea of where to start.

Q **You lead me to believe that I am on an endless quest and will be buying things forever. Have I misread your intention?**

How did it go?

A *No...*

Q **I don't mean to be rude, but isn't that quite a daunting prospect?**

A *No – look on it as an opportunity. It will give all shopping trips a purpose.*

Q **But if I collect pieces over time, they won't all necessarily match, will they?**

A *No, but I don't see that as a problem. I have been present at a dinner party where all the crockery and fine china was blue and white. The dinner plates varied in size and the side plates varied in shape, but walking into the room and seeing the sheer variety of items was a real treat. It was fresh and fun and nowhere near as much of a mishmash as you might think.*

43

Hens and stags

It's time for the engaged couple to party ... apart.

Tradition dictates that before you get married, you go out with friends of the same sex.

These occasions have always left me perplexed. Are they intended to be a celebration that you are still single or a lament that you will soon be answerable to another person? Why is it necessary to go out with all the boys, or girls, one last time? Unless you are going to have a very strange marriage and never let your partner out of your sight, then surely you will both be seeing your same-sex friends for a regular night out?

Hmm. Let's concentrate on the 'how to' rather than the 'why'.

(And why is the girls' night called a *hen* night? They are fussy, clucky, picky, put-upon birds. The boys' night is a *stag* night. The stag is a bold, strong, awesome beast – it doesn't seem fair somehow – right, moving on...)

It usually falls to the best man or the chief bridesmaid, or the maid of honour, to organise the event. So if you have been asked to fulfil one of these roles – and if you've accepted – how do you plan a memorable event?

**A little advance planning about
transport home is no bad thing,
especially if people are likely to
be drunk. If you know that a
venue closes at a certain time
then pre-book cabs home for
everyone. Remember your
responsibility to the hen or stag:
you must get them home safely.**

There are certain things that should be written
in stone.
- Rule number one. It isn't a surprise, so
  check with the bride or groom who exactly
  should be asked to join in the fun.
- Rule number two. Be realistic about the
  cost.
- Rule number three. Never, ever, arrange it
  for the night before the wedding.

And then there are a lot of details that you will want to bear in mind. It is lovely to
receive a written invite. There is something a little off-putting about a round-robin
email; that suggests that the person arranging the do is too busy to make a real
effort on behalf of the bride/groom. Which, given that they have been asked to play
a major part in the wedding ceremony, is not a good sign. So put something in the
post.

Take time to consider the nature of the event. If you are planning a wild and risqué
night then let everyone who has been invited know your intent. This may not be
everybody's idea of fun so give people the opportunity to come along for early
drinks and then excuse themselves graciously if they want to. There is nothing
worse than having one person in the group cringe with embarrassment or watch
from a distance with a disapproving look on
their face. Tailor the event to the people who
are coming along; don't just assume that as it
is a hen/stag night that everyone will want to
get drunk and fall over.

Defining
idea... **'It's the friends you can call
up at 4 a.m. that matter.'**
MARLENE DIETRICH

190

Book everything in advance. This is really important if you intend to go to a nightclub after dinner or drinks. Speak to the club manager and make sure that you are on a list and will be allowed in. If you take a chance and just turn up you may, for any number of reasons, not gain entry. This is especially important for a group of men as some places make a policy of not allowing stag nights onto the premises. Play it safe and clear it beforehand, taking a note of the name, job title and – if available – direct line phone number of the person that you talk to.

If you plan on making a toast, see IDEA 36, 'Here's looking at you, kid...'

Try another idea...

On the day you should confirm any bookings that you have made. Charge your mobile. Check that everyone who is coming along has your phone number and confirm the arrangements for the place and time that you are meeting. Use this as an opportunity to remind them about the projected cost, remembering that you will all plan to pay for the bride or groom.

And remember those rules I said should be engraved in granite earlier!

One last one. As the organiser of the event, you are charged with the responsibility of looking after the hen or stag. I know that it is unrealistic to ask you to remain sober but do try to stay two or three drinks behind the rest of the group.

'My friends, no matter how rough the road may be, we can and we will, never, never surrender to what is right.'
DAN QUAYLE, making what sounds like a typical stag party speech...

Defining idea...

There you have it. The responsibility is all yours; don't let your best friend down.

How did it go?

Q   We are all sworn to secrecy. What do you want to know?

A   If you don't need help, no problem.

Q   So you aren't offended?

A   No, really. It was probably quite tame compared to my hen night.

Q   Seriously though, I did wonder whether I had asked too many people along as we lost a few along the way. Is it better to keep numbers down?

A   My first question would be whether the bride/groom expected to see all the people that were present at the start. If they did, then the numbers were right. If they said afterwards 'I can't believe X and Y were there, I don't know them that well', then maybe you didn't do enough fine-tuning on the guest list. Listen, on any evening when there is a large group going out together, people will drift off when they have either a) drunk enough to know it's time to get home before they embarrass themselves or their host, or b) have found someone to chat up and got distracted. The fact that you lose a few along the way is nothing to worry about.

44

The good guest guide

Or how to be sure that your friends will stay in touch after you've been their guest!

Hospitality is a warm and wonderful thing. It should be appreciated and treated with the respect that it deserves.

So you have received an invitation. Then start as you mean to go on in your role as a model guest. If it requires an RSVP, respond quickly. When you have been asked to confirm dates, get your diary out and make the phone call.

There are a whole host of situations when you can impress people with your good manners.

THE DINNER PARTY GUEST

Always take a small gift with you when you have been invited to someone's home for a meal. I'm not talking about the occasions when a friend says, 'Drop by to watch the game and I'll make a pot of chilli', though clearly in this situation you would be expected to bring beer.

It's the more formal 'sit down around the table' meals that I'm referring to. It can be something really obvious, like a bottle of wine, or something that suggests that you

Here's an idea for you...

If you were dragged up properly then you should already know this, but don't be a slob when you are staying overnight. Leave the bedroom looking reasonably tidy at all times. Your host shouldn't really go in there unless you 'invite' them, but you don't want to risk them walking in on a complete tip. The same applies to the bathroom. If you spray toothpaste up the mirror then be sure to wipe it away before you leave.

have put some thought into it. If you know that the person who invited you loves to cook, for example, then pick up a bottle of fine olive oil or a selection of unusual spices. Do not arrive more than half an hour after the stated time and, at the other end of the evening, don't outstay your welcome. If you have to cancel for whatever reason, give plenty of notice so that the table setting can be rearranged and cooking amounts adjusted accordingly.

THE OVERNIGHT GUEST

Confirm your arrival time. Again arrive with a gift. As you will be fed more than once, consider taking a selection of fine cheeses or a fruit basket, something that will supplement the provisions in the house. When you arrive, let your host direct events. If that sounds obvious here's how you could go wrong. You ring the doorbell, receive a welcome and then say 'I'll get my bag out of the car so that I can take it up to my room.' No. You don't get to direct the action. Greet your host, enter the house and, at some point, they will suggest that they show you where you are to sleep: then you go and collect your bits and pieces from the car. And don't call an hour before you are due at the house to ask if you should bring anything with you. Your host will already have planned the meals and drinks by then; check with them the day before. It will give them time to think if there is anything you could pick up on the way.

Defining idea...

'Manners are especially the need of the plain. The pretty can get away with anything.'
EVELYN WAUGH

194

THE RESTAURANT GUEST

Are you a smoker? See IDEA 13, *Smoke signals*, **for some tips on good etiquette.**

Try another idea...

Car accidents or the receipt of terrible news aside, never excuse yourself from a restaurant meal if there are less than a few hours until you are due to eat. It's just rude. If you have not eaten there before, then check beforehand about the style of the restaurant and make sure that you dress accordingly. If you are a vegetarian or have any special dietary needs then make sure that your host is aware of this; it is then up to them to make sure that there are suitable dishes on the menu. If you are in any doubt about whether you are expected to contribute to the meal, try and sort this out beforehand. For example, if someone has asked you on the occasion of their partner's birthday, then it is perfectly all right to ask 'Are we all going to chip in and cover the cost of Chris's meal?'

As you start each course, try and keep pace with those eating on either side of you. Don't devour your food like a starving dog; you want to chat as you eat so allow time between mouthfuls. Do not reach for the wine bottle and fill up your own glass first; if it is formal then you must wait for the host to offer the bottle. If it is more relaxed, by all means pick up the bottle but top up everyone else's glass before you get to yours. On that note, moderate your alcohol intake according to the mood of the event. Never, ever, be the only dipsy tipsy person at the table.

Be a good guest and you'll be asked back time and again. If the invitations have dried up you need to smarten up your act!

'*A man who exposes himself when he is intoxicated, has not the art of getting drunk.*'
SAMUEL JOHNSON

Defining idea...

How did it go?

Q   I forgot to bring a gift for the weekend, what should I do now?

A   *Shame on you. However, all is not lost. Why not suggest that you would like to buy your hosts Sunday lunch to say thanks for their hospitality?*

Q   That would be fine but we are expecting other guests here for Sunday lunch so all the supplies have been bought. I can't afford to pay for everyone! Any other suggestions?

A   *See, this is what happens when you forget something in the first place. It all gets a lot more complicated. Why not suggest that you go out for a drink before lunch and make sure that you get to the bar first. If there is a special occasion attached to your visit, then why not buy a bottle of champagne and return to the table with that? It will come as a lovely surprise. And next time, remember.*

45

Guess who's coming to dinner?

You need to plan a menu and put together a formal dinner party for the boss...

When the occasion calls for fine food, the best wine and a beautifully dressed table, it's important that nothing gets rushed.

If you have been employed by the same company for any length of time, the chances are that you will have spent a certain amount of time socialising with your boss. Whether it's office drinks, client cocktail parties or company family days, some events are business-related and others purely social. What can happen at the family occasions, is that your partner can land you in it...

Here's the scenario. You introduce your partner to your boss's partner and you quickly realise that they have a lot more in common than you and your boss. So much so that your partner says to the other person, 'Why don't you both come over to our house next weekend?' Once the invitation is out there, you can't take it back. After you've confirmed the details and moved on with a polite excuse, you then take your partner away to a quiet corner and smack them sharply round the back of the head. Then you start to panic.

Here's an idea for you...

If the prospect of cooking a dinner for your boss and having them in your house for several hours fills you with fear and trepidation, there is an easy alternative. Arrange to have cocktails instead. Issue an invite that gives a very specific time range: 'Come for drinks between seven and nine.' Then if things are going well at 9 p.m., you can allow it to drift on. However, if it has been a bit of a minefield full of social gaffes, you can give the wink to a couple of friends and get them to instigate the winding up of the event.

(And if you don't, then you're not normal.)

Right, the first thing is: don't let the idea scare you. It had to happen at some point and at least this way you'll get it over with. Who knows, you might even enjoy it so much that you repeat it in the future... hmm. Seriously, just think how much good it might do your career if your boss sees the sparkling, entertaining, relaxed, amusing, witty individual that is concealed behind your tough, serious, stressed-out work persona.

The first thing to plan is who else to invite along and what sort of meal to prepare. Try to avoid making it an entirely work affair. If a few of your closest friends can be trusted not to embarrass you then include them, plus one or two work colleagues with whom you enjoy socialising. If everyone that you are planning to ask has children, then why not make it a family barbecue? There are plenty of distractions with kids around and everyone can get involved with burning the burgers and tossing the salad. This makes for a relaxing environment, even considering that the boss is there. Who knows, maybe they have hidden barbecuing talents and will be in their element? If you can't rely on the weather, then still ask families over but arrange to host a buffet instead. If your boss doesn't have children, then don't make it a child-friendly affair. Arrange a dinner party or evening buffet.

PERFECT PLANNING

There is no question that you are probably
going to be nervous at the prospect of the boss
coming to dinner, and a sunken soufflé, a corked bottle of wine, a set of linen that
isn't ironed or a messy bunch of flowers should all be avoided.

So you want to impress the
boss. See IDEA 46, *The perfect
host*, for some useful advice.

Try another idea...

The point of the occasion is either to impress or get to know the person and to do
that you need to be relaxed. For that to be the case, I would strongly recommend
that you do not attempt to cook anything very tricky (no soufflé) or anything that
could go wrong at the last minute. Stick to recipes that you know look good and are
almost guaranteed to come out right every time. Another important point to bear
in mind is that you do not want to be stuck in the kitchen all night. The point of
the occasion is to spend time with the boss, so it would be good to include one or
two courses on your menu that can be prepared in advance.

This is why it can make sense to have a buffet; you'll only need to disappear when
you want to clear plates or restock platters. The other advantage is that people can
mingle and move around and you can probably accommodate a few more guests.

Who knows, you might actually enjoy yourself!

*'Nothing ever comes to one,
that is worth having, except
as a result of hard work.'*
BOOKER T. WASHINGTON

Defining idea...

How did it go?

Q **My boss and his wife are a lot older than we are. Is it still fine to ask my friends along?**

A *Yes of course, but do include a few people from work who bridge the age gap so that the balance isn't tipped too far towards the younger generation.*

Q **I show a lot of respect to him at work but how casual can I be at home?**

A *I would say be deferential but don't grovel. Let your boss sit down first at the table and hold the chair out for his wife. Ask him if he would like to taste the wine before you pour – but only with the first bottle. Make sure that his wife is served first with the food, but then it must go to all the other women at the table before he gets his plate.*

46

The perfect host

You're in charge, and you have everyone under your control. That kind of thinking can get you into all sorts of trouble.

Having guests is not a chance for you to boss people around!

When you are the host (or hostess, but I'll use 'host' to cover both sexes from now on) the idea is for people to feel relaxed around you and not jump to attention every time you make a movement, scared to put a foot – or say a word – out of place. Here's how to get it right.

When people are coming to stay for more than one night, you really want them to be able to treat your home as their own, so let them have a set of keys. If you do not already have a spare set, make sure that you get them cut before your guests arrive. You don't want it to appear like a last-minute, inconvenient chore as that sends out totally the wrong message about your intentions. Guests who have the freedom to come and go at their own behest will be far more relaxed then those who feel that they are tied in to your schedule. (The obvious scenario would be when you have to go to work while they are staying. You don't want to drag them out of bed at eight in the morning just because that's when you need to leave.)

Here's an idea for you...

While you may want to have dinner ready on the first night of their arrival, especially if they have travelled a long way, don't feel that you have to wait on your guests and cook every meal. Involve them in the preparation and clearing up at meal times. It is perfectly acceptable to say 'I am making a spaghetti sauce, would one of you like to come and chop the onions for me?' or 'I'm going to put this lot in the dishwasher, could you give me a hand to get everything stacked, then we can have coffee...'

Do you live near to public transport? Then make a list of possible buses, trams or trains that might be of use if they want to go sightseeing while they are staying with you. A little basic orientation is a help. Have a local map handy, and make sure your guests know exactly where your house is located, so that they can find their own way around without having to ask you every time they plan a trip out.

Prepare your home so that both they and you can relax. Yes, that does involve a spring clean! If you are worried about the appalling state of the bathroom or the chaos that reigns in the kitchen, you won't be happy to let them roam around your home at will. Worse, if you leave them alone in the house, they might feel an obligation to start tidying up in case they feel that they have had added an extra burden to your usual household chores.

Defining idea...

'Guests, like fish, begin to smell after three days.'
BENJAMIN FRANKLIN

In an ideal world, there is a spare room available for them. If that isn't the case, then try and make their temporary accommodation as comfortable as possible. If you don't have a sofa bed in the lounge, for example, then buy a really good quality inflatable mattress that will provide them with a decent night's sleep.

A beautifully prepared guest bathroom is a real treat. Check out IDEA 26, *Bathing beauties*.

Try another idea...

Are they bringing a baby? This is where good hosting can make a real difference to their trip. If you can, borrow a cot so that they do not have to pack one. If you can find out what kind of nappies they use, then providing a pack will relieve them of any pressure should they arrive and realise supplies are low. Clear a space on the work surface and a shelf in a kitchen cupboard where they can put the steriliser or stack jars of baby food. If all the kit and caboodle that is required for feeding the baby can be kept in one place, it will be much more relaxing for them than having to drag stuff in and out of a baby bag. If you have a pet that is not used to children, warn them of its presence in advance. Much as your surrogate child might usually rule the roost, plan to confine the animal to certain areas, leaving some rooms animal-free for the first few hours of their stay. Initially introduce your pet to your guests and then gradually allow it to roam once they are settled. Never leave an animal alone with a small child, however friendly you think it might be.

Above all, consideration for your guests – and any gestures that will contribute to their enjoyment of the stay – will make you the host with the most.

'*House guests should be regarded as perishables: leave them out too long and they go bad.*'
ERMA BOMBECK, author

Defining idea...

Q   **I have decided to put together an itinerary for when my guests arrive so that they have plenty of things to keep them occupied. That's a good idea, right?**

A   *Hmm. Are you doing this for their benefit or your own? If you are using it as an excuse to visit all the sights that you have never got around to seeing, you might want to consider whether they have come for some rest and relaxation.*

Q   **You mean I don't get to play tour guide?**

A   *Hey, it's up to you. But I would suggest that in place of an itinerary, you gather together information on all the different activities that are available and let them decide how often they want to go out. They may be coming to see you with the intention of de-stressing themselves on your sofa and working their way through your collection of DVDs.*

47

The wine club

Holding a tasting party is the perfect way to combine fun with learning.

A little knowledge is a good thing, and when it comes to wine it can make all the difference.

Yes, that's the difference between knocking back a jug of the house red or savouring the flavours in a carefully selected bottle, chosen for the renowned qualities of its grapes. But there are things you should know before you start.

If you don't know a vintage from a variety – and are clueless about the meaning of 'appellation' start here:

Vintage: the grape harvest of a particular year.

Variety: the kind of grapes used. Certain wines don't list the variety because the law states that wines from a designated appellation must be made from particular varieties of grapes. For example, if a wine carries the Chablis appellation, it will be made of Chardonnay grapes – so there's no need to list that on the label.

Appellation: the name of the region in which a particular grape is grown. This can be a state (such as California), an area (Bordeaux, in France) or the vineyard.

Winery: not always there, but indicates the people who produced or bottled it.

Here's an idea for you... If you need to choose wines for a particular party or an event such as a wedding, you have the perfect excuse to hold a wine tasting. It is good to get a range of opinions on what wine will best suit the people that have been invited to the event and it also allows you to taste wines that fall into different price brackets. You can then allocate more or less of your budget to the wine, depending on how important you feel it is to the occasion.

MAKING A CHOICE

How do you decide which wines to drink? You can make your selection based on any number of variables but how about one of the following?

- By grape. Try tasting different Chardonnays from across the globe. It is bottled in a number of different countries, each of which will produce a variety of characteristics.
- By price. This is my favoured option because it is amazing how many times a cheaper, supermarket-sourced bottle stands up very well against a much more expensive wine that has been bought from a specialist wine merchant.
- By different wine makers within a region: for example, you could taste a number of same-grape wines (varietals) from different makers in the Napa Valley.

I would recommend that you choose a minimum of five bottles. That gives everyone who comes the chance to appreciate a good range. By all means buy as many bottles as you want but bear in mind that when you hold a tasting party at home, a lot of people will drink all of the wine you pour rather than taste and then spit. And on that note, professional wine tasters discovered long ago that by the time they had savoured several bottles, they wouldn't be fit to write the notes if they drank each sample. That's why they spit. (If any of your guests are reluctant to

spit into a bucket on the grounds of good
manners, point out to them that it would be
far worse etiquette to swallow everything that
is poured and then throw up in the bucket.
This convinces all but the most stubborn
drinkers.)

**Get together a collection of the
right glasses for the drinks
involved: see IDEA 30, *The
class of glass.***

*Try
another
idea...*

At the first few attempts people will consume much more than is really necessary,
so be sure to provide some snacks to soak up the effects of the alcohol. Breadsticks
or plain crackers are ideal during the tasting but save anything more exotic until
afterwards as anything with a strong flavour will affect your appreciation of the
wine.

REACH FOR THE CORKSCREW

Here are some important pointers for your
tasting:

*'Wine is constant proof that
God loves us and loves to see
us happy.'*
BENJAMIN FRANKLIN

*Defining
idea...*

- Make sure that you serve the wine at the
  correct temperature – you'll find these listed on any good wine merchant's
  website.
- Allow red wine time to breathe.
- When the wine is ready, only fill glasses about a third of the way up the bowl.
- Once everybody has a glass, hold them up to the light and compare descriptions
  of the colour. You can just talk about everything but it is much more fun to give
  everyone a notebook, ask them to write down their thoughts and then swap so
  that nobody reads out their own notes. This provokes a much livelier discussion.
- Next, you want to savour the bouquet – so swirl the wine around the bowl and
  then insert your nose and inhale.

- Lastly, take a sip. Allow the liquid to sit on your tongue and roll it around in your mouth for several seconds.
- Spit or swallow…

And before you try the next bottle, make sure that the glasses have been washed out and dried, and that everyone has cleared their palate with a mouthful of water.

Now grab the bottles and start your swilling and sniffing.

How did it go?

Q   When we read out the notes we realised that we might need some help with verbalising our impressions of the wines. What do you say?

A   It sounds like a good plan. Try some of these. I have suggested them in the context of red or white but feel free to interchange them. Red wines can be blowsy, pungent or have a hint of chocolate or blackcurrant. White wines can be tart (without being promiscuous), nutty, dry and have an underlying hint of gooseberry and oak.

Q   Do I really need to look in a thesaurus?

A   It's as good a starting point as any. Look under 'fruit', look under 'flavour', look under 'colour' – well, that's three places to get you started. Keep this up and you'll have a wonderfully lyrical description for every bottle that you try.

48

Side by side

Put the perfect seating plan in place.

When you are part of the planning process for a formal event, one of the most challenging tasks can be to position people in the right place.

What do I mean when I say 'right'? well, it's a combination of tradition, expectation and pandering to egos in order to ensure that guests are happy with their designated seat. If that sounds to you like a diplomatic minefield, then you are right. Understand the importance of planning it carefully and bear in mind that you should endeavour to meet everyone's expectations.

FIND A SEAT

Your starting point is the guest list. While you can make a stab at putting everyone in a particular place, it is only when all the RSVPs have been received that you can finalise the table plan. Try and make an objective assessment of the people that will be present. Think about any who are already good friends and consider whether there are any enemies among the guests. Will a divorced or recently separated couple be attending alone or each be bringing their new partners? Is there someone who is good-humoured enough to get along with anyone, or who can be trusted to

Here's an idea for you...

Acknowledge that your guests will want to move around and meet or greet people that have been placed in different parts of the room. Take away any uncertainty on their part about when it's acceptable to move by making sure that this is mentioned at the end of a speech or toast. For example: 'We hope that you will take the opportunity before the dancing starts to mingle with other guests.'

make conversation with anybody, even the most boring person? Maybe you could even help romance blossom because you know that two individuals have expressed an interest in each other. Finally, appreciate that good friends, if seated in close proximity, will egg each other on to accept dare after dare.

So now you understand what I mean when I say that a good seating plan is a challenge!

Thankfully some situations, the more formal ones, can be easy to address. The seating plan for the top table at a wedding for example, should follow the accepted form: from left to right – chief bridesmaid, groom's father, bride's mother, groom, bride, bride's father, groom's mother, best man.

Right, now let's consider situations where there is no 'accepted' order. From christenings to golden wedding anniversaries, if a formal dinner is part of the celebration then use the following suggestions as a guide:

- Immediate family and close friends should be closest to the top table.
- Other relatives should be placed at the next nearest tables.
- Good friends (people who will themselves acknowledge that they are part of the group but not at the core) deserve to be next.

Defining idea...

'Plans are nothing; planning is everything.'
DWIGHT D. EISENHOWER

- Juggle the remaining guests as you see fit. However, try to plan that people who are known to each other will be together; the exception are those people who will be a bad influence on each other!

If you are going to a party on your own, see IDEA 35, *All by myself.*

Try another idea...

It is customary to alternate men and women around the table. My advice is to stick with tradition. People will move around once the final course has been served and sit where they are comfortable.

ADVANCE WARNING

Arrange to have a printed table plan positioned just outside the dining area. This gives everyone the chance to peruse it before they sit down and speeds up the process when you ask people to take their seats. It should be drawn up to mirror the appearance of the room. By that I mean that if the tables are round you use circles, and if they are square or oblong, you feature the appropriate shape. List the names of everyone allocated to each table in alphabetical order. Use place cards on the table itself to indicate each person's seat. If guests choose to rearrange these to suit themselves, then so be it. You have done your job.

No one can guarantee that everyone will click with their companions at the table, but combine a complementary mix of people and you are setting up a situation full of potential.

'At a formal dinner party, the person nearest death should always be seated closest to the bathroom.'
GEORGE CARLIN, US comedian

Defining idea...

213

Q **It's a tricky one. I don't really know everyone well enough to guarantee that friends are seated with friends, so how can I be sure of keeping everyone happy?**

A *I'm going to add to your workload. Please dedicate time to talk to some of the invited guests. Try to get a feel for the character of one or two of the individuals with whom you are not acquainted. If you get the impression that one person is always the life and soul of the party, then team them with a group that may benefit from a bit of fun.*

Q **Should I call people and give them a choice of tables when I draw up the seating plan?**

A *That's not a bad idea. But do try to prevent a clique forming that could become the focus of attention when it's someone else's special day.*

Q **How do you mean?**

A *Here's an example. I once went to a wedding where one of the tables was allocated to a group of friends who had all been at university with the groom. The noise from that table grew and grew as the wine flowed. By the time it came to the speeches, they heckled and shouted and generally became the focus of everyone's attention, which should have been directed towards the top table. I felt at the time, and I still do, that if the eight couples had been split up – say four together on one table and four at another – with other people to chat to with whom they would have shared no in-jokes, then they might have been a little more sympathetic towards everyone else at the wedding. And to their friend the groom, of course.*

49

A touch of romance

Make plans to indulge the one you love.

Ask yourself this. Can you remember the last time when you ignored all other distractions, and focused your attention entirely on your partner?

If you can't recall anything at all or are having trouble remembering where and when this last happened, then maybe it's time to address the situation!

Typically when we talk about entertaining, it implies that we're planning an event for a group of people. But why not aim to restrict the guest list to just one name? If you are in a relationship, then taking time to entertain your other half might be worth a little thought, especially if it will come as a complete surprise. Romance has a different meaning for everyone so I cannot give you hard and fast rules. Will you accept a suggestion? Fine; then consider the following idea: plan an alternative to your usual routine. That can manifest itself in any number of different ways. But it is a useful starting point from which you can work.

Would you like an example? Skip the usual Friday night trip to the movies with the girls. Be at home with cocktails mixed when he gets home. Opt out of the regular boys' night down the pub; have a take-away ordered and a bottle of bubbly chilling in the fridge as a surprise.

Here's an idea for you... **You want to impress but it is a good idea to keep things simple so that pretty much everything can be prepared in advance. There is nothing more annoying than having to break off in the middle of an intimate conversation so that you can rush into the kitchen to take a dish off the hob. The less you have to worry about preparing and organising after your partner has joined you, the better.**

It doesn't take a lot of thought to do something unexpected. And quite often something unexpected, however simple it may be, is as romantic as a huge, overblown gesture.

Plan to do the following things:

- Issue an invitation. Put a note in their wallet or handbag that they will only find when they have left the house. It will be discovered when they are rummaging for their travel ticket or searching for change to pay for the morning coffee.
- Remove the distractions. If you have kids, arrange for a family member or close friend to take the children overnight.
- Allow yourself plenty of time to set up the surprise before they are due on the scene.

Now, plan an icebreaker to begin the evening. While you have been thinking about this for some time, for your partner it's recent news and they may need something to put them in the mood (and perhaps stop them being suspicious). Run a lovely bubble bath and light

Defining idea... **'If love is the answer, could you rephrase the question?'**
LILY TOMLIN

candles in the room. Direct your partner
upstairs as soon as they get home and after a
few minutes, when you have given them time
to undress and get in the bath, deliver a glass of

Do you want to toast your loved one? See IDEA 36, *'Here's looking at you, kid...'*

Try another idea...

chilled champagne. (By now you may be in the mood for a 'little fine loving' but
control your libido and do not jump on them in the bath. Leave them to savour
some relaxing time alone and they will be all the more eager to join in with the
spirit of the surprise when they have had time to relax.)

Plan to serve their favourite food and surprise them with a gift in between each
course. Don't drink so much that you both get very weary and fall asleep, that's not
the idea.

If you are in the mood for love, there is one thing that could really dampen your
partner's enthusiasm – mess. If you sweep someone off to the
bedroom/bathroom/sofa, only to have them surrounded by the usual household
detritus – newspapers strewn across the floor, dirty mugs on the coffee table – then
nothing you do will work. Please make the time to tidy up; even if it is just a
superficial job and you chuck everything in a cupboard, at least it makes a change
from the usual chaos. Remember that seeing a pile of dirty laundry at the end of
the bed will act like a mental bucket of ice-cold
water to many people. Take the time to remake
the bed, maybe change it and – yes, you got it,
tidy up...

'Men also have to be
seductive – and with men it
is more difficult because it is
not in their education.'
JEAN-PAUL GAULTIER

Defining idea...

217

How did it go?

Q **Well, the plans are in place but I am not sure what to wear. Should I put on a suit?**

A *I love seeing a man in a suit, and if you were going out for the evening, then I would say yes. However if you are spending the evening at home, you really want to be relaxed, so wear something casual.*

Q **Surely it will look like I haven't made much of an effort. Won't she think I'm a scruff?**

A *I am sure that your other half will have commented that you look especially good in a particular T-shirt or pair of form-fitting jeans. Wear an outfit that you have been complemented on in the past – it is a real winner if they haven't seen you wearing it for a while.*

Q **She likes to prepare well in advance for most things so does it matter that she won't have planned an outfit for this?**

A *If that worries you then buy her something new to wear, wrap it up and leave the parcel in the middle of your (beautifully made) bed. That way she doesn't have to worry about rummaging through the wardrobe to find something suitable. Just a note: don't buy sultry lingerie unless it the type of thing that she would choose to wear. And if you do, get the size right. Many a great idea has been ruined by poor research!*

50

Scary stuff

Halloween is the one night of the year when you are fully entitled to behave badly.

Although I am not a huge fan of 'trick or treating', I am all in favour of everyone donning crazy outfits, putting on mad make-up and going a bit wild.

Maybe it's my upbringing or my formative years, but I think it is quite acceptable for individuals of any sex, whatever their age, to dress up. *ET*, the film, also has a lot to answer for. Remember the scene when Drew Barrymore dresses up and ET is put in a hat? (If you don't know what I am talking about then get the video now. It will all become clear when you watch the film.)

Halloween offers the perfect excuse for some silly antics. Let's face it, while some entertainment has to be organised and formal (you need to look neat and tidy and you need to be on your best behaviour) a party taking place on this night gives everyone an excuse to act up.

Here's an idea for you...

Combine a party with the trick or treating part of the day. Ask two or three of your friends with children to come over in the early evening and get the kids dressed up while you don outfits too. You can share the make-up, which means you get to paint the kids' faces, and in return, they get to transform you. When they know that there are these kinds of fun and games at home, they will be eager to do the trick or treat run in record time and the sooner you can settle down and know that they are safely at home, the better.

Now, what are the elements of a well-planned Halloween party?

- Outrageous outfits (including the obligatory white sheets with holes cut in the appropriate places – for the eyes, that is!).
- Good quality, scary make-up.
- Horrendous masks.
- Black or orange food.
- Fireworks.
- Pumpkins.
- Candles.
- Spray cobwebs.
- A selection of scary films.

Call me a child, but this has all the elements of a really good time.

TRICK OR TREAT?

As I have already said, I don't warm to the idea of trick or treating. If you are going to let your children go out and do this, then please either accompany them or lay down some really strict guidelines like these. Visit houses within the neighbourhood, preferably where you know the residents, and don't assume that everyone likes the idea; they must avoid frightening anyone unnecessarily. An elderly person, for example, might not appreciate a knock on the door late in the evening. And grumpy people (like myself) ignore the door. If people don't answer the first time you ring the bell, respect their privacy. Always travel in a group. Meet up with other children in the area so you pay your neighbours one visit, as opposed to lots of smaller groups knocking on their door throughout the evening.

You might want to mix up some cocktails on Halloween; see IDEA 8, *The cocktail-hour kit*, and IDEA 9, *Stocking up*, on where to start.

Try another idea...

PUT ON A SHOW

So you have decided to celebrate with a few friends at your house. If ever a day called for ridiculous decorations and over the top entertainment, this is it. If ever an occasion demanded that you dress up, this is it.

Dress up your home too; use an orange and black colour scheme. Have carved pumpkins as focal points for the buffet, the drinks table and, if the weather is good enough, to illuminate the garden. Don't be shy of making generous use of cobweb spray, rubber bats and the occasional fake spider; put them in the windows, hanging over doors or in places where people would least expect them. For example, a spider stuck to the wall just by the light pull for the bathroom will guarantee a few screams.

'There is nothing funny about Halloween. This sarcastic festival reflects, rather, an infernal demand for revenge by children on the adult world.'
JEAN BAUDRILLARD

Defining idea...

221

Defining
idea...

'Charlie Brown is the one person I identify with. C.B. is such a loser. He wasn't even the star of his own Halloween special.'
CHRIS ROCK, US comedian

WHAT SHOULD YOU WEAR?

Listen, if you can't work that out then you need to read a few fairy stories or watch some classic films and TV programmes. *Dracula, Frankenstein, The Addams Family, Spider-man, The Wizard of Oz, Buffy, The Munsters* – take your pick. If you think you might want to hire your costume, then plan in advance – good ones go quickly.

AND THE GAMES?

Regardless of their age, everyone should be forced to play Bob the Apple at a Halloween party. If you have a mix of children and grown-ups, put a fair selection of ages on each team. Another great way to entertain a group of young kids and adults is to hold a pumpkin-carving competition.

Fear not, if you allow yourself to indulge all of your most juvenile fantasies, your Halloween party will be a blast!

Q Well, I've got the games organised but I am stumped as to what I should do with the food and drink. Can you help?

How did it go?

A Let me give you a few pointers. Serve punch from a cauldron, put bread in an inverted witch's hat, make pumpkin soup or even experiment with blue and red food colouring to create 'bloodthirsty' cakes.

Q This all sounds quite disgusting, are you sure?

A Oh, yes. Put aside all your preconceptions about beautifully presented food and tasteful drinks and let your imagination run riot. I can virtually guarantee that when you have put a lot of time and effort into a Halloween party – and seen the shock, horror and amazement on the faces of your grown-up friends and their offspring – that you will look forward to next year when they will have to rise to the challenge of being scarier than you.

51

Family fun

It's time to entertain your nearest and dearest, so make it a pleasure, not a chore.

Well, it's your turn to host the annual gathering of the clan...

The house is immaculate. The meals are already planned. There are games for the children to play and drinks for the adults; you've even got the right nibbles all ready. In fact you are perfectly prepared, so what could upset these brilliantly executed plans?

However much you love your kith and kin, conflicts can arise for any number of reasons. Say, for example, that you have spent hours in the kitchen putting together a fantastic meal. Your big sister walks in and offers a 'helpful' suggestion that will make your roast potatoes taste just as good as the ones that she cooks at home. Because you have spent hours preparing the food, you are a trifle hot and bothered, so you snap back an answer. She takes offence and you, full of self-righteous indignation, are not going to apologise. It's a silly situation but neither of you will admit that you are in the wrong.

Entertaining the family can be stressful, so here are a few suggestions that might help you enjoy rather than endure your time together.

Here's an idea for you...

I've often noticed that it's amazing how quickly children become fascinated with old black and white pictures of previous generations, especially if one of the older members of the family can contribute anecdotes about the life and times of the people shown. They also love to see pictures of their parents when they were children. Can you gather together old pictures and albums and set aside time for everyone to sit down together and look through these?

- Try to maintain a sense of humour. Your parents' annoying habit of always bickering might not seem so irritating if you don't take it too seriously.
- Accept that you can't control someone else's behaviour. Even if you do not approve when your adolescent nephew refuses to join in a game, it is up to his parents to deal with the situation.
- Don't miss out on sleep. If you are tired you are more likely to be oversensitive and irritable.
- Give everyone some space. Arrange your home so that there is a quiet room where people can read, a place for the kids and a TV area so that people who want to watch a particular programme can do so.
- Leave the house. Make a trip to the supermarket or simply disappear for a walk – it will give people time to relax without the host's presence.
- Be flexible with your normal schedule. You may always eat breakfast at 9 a.m. and then clear up the kitchen, but let your family drift down to eat in the morning whenever they are ready. Don't panic if toast and juice is lying around most of the morning.

Defining idea...

'The greatest thing in family life is to take a hint when a hint is intended – and not to take a hint when a hint isn't intended.'
ROBERT FROST, US poet

THE GENERATION GAP

See IDEA 32, *And the kids came too*, if you are taking your children to an event.

Try another idea...

One of the biggest challenges when the family gets together is meeting the needs of people of widely differing ages. How do you entertain a grandparent at the same time as occupying a teenager?

Children tend to become noisy and disruptive when they are bored. Older relatives like a bit of peace and the chance to grab a catnap when they are tired so try and be prepared to accommodate their respective needs. If you can organise an outing for the youngsters after lunch, it means that the house will be quiet for a while and give the senior members of the family a chance to relax in peace.

RESOLVING CONFLICT

So you have a disagreement with someone and the atmosphere is tense. The last thing that you want to do is let the situation drag on and on. Choose a time and location when there will be no other distractions; discuss the issue and keep the conversation to the specific incident that upset you rather than launch into a list of long-held grievances. In my experience, it really helps to diffuse the conflict if you can speak quietly and in a calm and considered way. Another important point is to make sure that you hear the other person out – listen to what they have to say without interrupting them in mid-sentence.

Finally be willing to compromise. Meet them halfway if it will mean a quick resolution to the quarrel.

'A family's photograph album is generally about the extended family and, often, is all that remains of it.'
SUSAN SONTAG

Defining idea...

They're your family for life – so enjoy!

How did
it go?

Q **I'm not sure that I can cope with having the family at my place, is there another option?**

A *Yes, of course. Break with tradition and book a restaurant instead. Sometimes it is easier to keep everyone happy when you are on neutral territory. No one can criticise your cooking or your decor and there are plenty of distractions that will provide subjects for conversations.*

Q **But what if they indulge in their usual hobby of deliberately winding each other up?**

A *There is a strong possibility that because they are out in public, they will resist the temptation to provoke an embarrassing situation. However, because you are not at home, you always have the option of deciding it is time to leave and can make a graceful exit, leaving them to fight it out among themselves.*

52

The last goodbye

Some things to consider when you need to plan a funeral.

I can pass on some suggestions and offer a little guidance, but of all the events that you will have to plan in your life, this is the most difficult on which to give definitive advice.

As so much depends upon the age of the person, the cause of their death and their situation in life, every funeral is unique. Also depending on their religion, there will be different traditions to which you must adhere. They may also have held strong personal views which you need to consider. There are plenty of occasions when the deceased will have left specific instructions about what they wish to happen after their death. It removes a considerable amount of stress if you have no doubt that they would like to be buried or cremated, or even wished to donate their body to science. But many times death comes without warning, or the person who died failed to be specific, and then you are left to decide.

As an alternative to people sending flowers in memory of the deceased, why not state that there will be family flowers at the funeral and ask people to make a donation to a charity instead, in the name of the person who has just died?

Discuss this with close relatives and ask for their opinions. Speak to intimate friends. They may at some point over the years have had a 'late night' discussion about this particular situation. Since my eldest brother was killed in an accident, I have made a point of letting people know my preferences and I think many people do the same at some point in their lives, so don't be afraid of asking around.

So, who will take care of the body? While it may sound strange to recommend that you shop around, it is really important that you feel totally comfortable with the people who are providing the funeral services. Please start by making phone calls and resist the temptation to go and visit several funeral homes, which can be distressing. Speak to however many people it takes until you feel you have found someone in whom you can put your trust and then arrange to go and see them. Even at this stage, if you have any misgivings at all then they will most certainly add to your unhappiness – don't feel pressured into making any arrangements until you are totally at ease. When you do make a visit, don't go alone. However strong you think that you are, you will need both emotional and physical support.

Defining idea...

'I didn't attend the funeral, but I sent a nice letter saying I approved of it.'
MARK TWAIN

Once you have made that decision, there are many other details to consider:
- What type of coffin would be right?
- Are you going to have a headstone?
- Do you wish to put a notice in a newspaper?

- What form will the funeral service take?
- Are you going to ask particular people to speak or give a reading or will you set aside time for anyone to give a spontaneous tribute?

If you are planning to raise a glass in memory, see IDEA 36, 'Here's looking at you, kid…' on making a toast.

Try another idea…

AFTER THE SERVICE

I've never attended an Irish wake but it seems to me that there is no better way to celebrate someone's life than to have a party in their honour. If they regularly drank in one particular pub or bar and were well known to the people that run it, then it could be the ideal venue for a drink after the funeral.

Of course, that might not be appropriate, in which case you may choose to ask people back to the family home after the service. In this situation, I would suggest that you put together a light buffet but don't feel that you have to prepare an amazing spread. Most people will pick up one or two sandwiches but it is rare for anyone to eat that much after a funeral.

Here's one piece of advice, which may sound a bit obvious, but it's really important. Try to ensure that all the organisation has been completed at least a couple of days before the funeral. You will be under an enormous amount of stress and will be grieving for the loss of a loved one. If you can spend the day before the funeral without having to make telephone calls to confirm arrangements it will give you a chance to be calm.

'Death is no more than passing from one room into another. But there's a difference for me, you know. Because in that other room I shall be able to see.'
HELEN KELLER

Defining idea…

231

How did
it go?

Q I would like to hold a wake. I know this may sound silly at a time like this but should I pay for everyone's drinks?

A *It is entirely up to you but I would suggest that you put a small amount of money behind the bar and let everyone know that once that has gone they will have to buy their own drinks.*

Q After all the funeral expenses, it will only be a modest amount. Is that all right?

A *Yes, that is absolutely fine, everyone will understand, just don't make a fuss about it. You may well find that other people add to the kitty as a gesture on the day.*

Q I would like to write a letter of condolence but I don't know where to start. Can you help?

A *This is one of the hardest things in the world. When my brother died, only one of my college friends, Howard, took the time to speak to my Mum about it, and he remains a treasured friend to this day. So it is important. I find it easiest just to say, or write, exactly what you are feeling. Be honest about your grief. It's far more important to send a letter or make a phone call, however badly you feel that you might have expressed yourself, than to simply ignore the situation and hope you can deal with it when you next meet the person to whom you wish to extend your condolences.*

The end...

Or is it a new beginning?

We hope that this book has inspired you to learn some new party tricks. Maybe you've organised a perfect family picnic, or a big formal dinner for all your partner's work colleagues (OK, bit of a long shot that one). When your friends arrive we hope they're knocked sideways by your inspired ideas and meticulous planning. And when they leave we know they'll have enjoyed an event they'll remember for ever. Let us know if that's the case. We'd like to be as amazed and impressed as they are.

So tell us how you got on. What did it for you – what helped you to throw a party that really fizzed? Maybe you've got some tips of your own you want to share (see next page if so). And if you liked this book you may find we have even more brilliant ideas that could change other areas of your life for the better.

You'll find the Infinite Ideas crew waiting for you online at www.infideas.com.

Or if you prefer to write, then send your letters to:
Perfect Parties
The Infinite Ideas Company Ltd
36 St Giles, Oxford OX1 3LD, United Kingdom

We want to know what you think, because we're all working on making our lives better too. Give us your feedback and you could win a copy of another *52 Brilliant Ideas* book of your choice. Or maybe get a crack at writing your own.

Good luck. Be brilliant.

Offer one

CASH IN YOUR IDEAS

We hope you enjoy this book. We hope it inspires, amuses, educates and entertains you. But we don't assume that you're a novice, or that this is the first book that you've bought on the subject. You've got ideas of your own. Maybe our author has missed an idea that you use successfully. If so, why not send it to yourauthormissedatrick@infideas.com, and if we like it we'll post it on our bulletin board. Better still, if your idea makes it into print we'll send you four books of your choice or the cash equivalent. You'll be fully credited so that everyone knows you've had another Brilliant Idea.

Offer two

HOW COULD YOU REFUSE?

Amazing discounts on bulk quantities of Infinite Ideas books are available to corporations, professional associations and other organisations.

For details call us on:
+44 (0)1865 514888
fax: +44 (0)1865 514777
or e-mail: info@infideas.com

Where it's at...

Even more brilliant ideas...

Secrets of wine

Giles Kime

"A few years ago I applied for a job on a wine magazine. 'Tell us about yourself,' said my prospective boss. 'Well, I don't really know much about wine,' I replied. I was offered the job anyway and I've spent almost every day since asking questions about wine. The only way to truly understand wine is by asking questions, and some of the answers will surprise you – not least that wine is far simpler to understand than you think."

"Forget the wine snobbery, the 'bouquet reminiscent of elderberries drying on a nun's bicycle seat' approach; this pretentious imagery seems to dominate the world of wine and the wine bores who spout such expressions all have one thing in common. Their heads are full of other people's ideas. In Secrets of wine I offer an insider's guide to the real world of wine ... the kind of advice that allows you to come up with your own thoughts. It's time for you to become a free-thinking drinker!" **Giles Kime**

Available from all good bookshops or call us on +44 (0)1865 514888

Create your dream garden

Jem Cook, Anna Marsden and Mark Hillsdon

"Don't worry. This isn't a garden makeover book that tries to convince you to put decking over every plant you see, nor will it teach you how to spot your Parthenocissus quinquefolia *or your* Convallaria majalis. Create your dream garden *is a practical insider's guide to getting the most from your garden."*

"You'll discover what's practical for you to achieve and most importantly what you can do that's (relatively) low maintenance. You won't end up with a degree in horticulture, but you will have a garden that delights and blooms!" **Jem Cook, Anna Marsden and Mark Hillsdon**